MAKE YOUR OWN

JAPANESE

CLOTHES

MAKE YOUR OWN
JAPANESE
CLOTHES

PATTERNS AND IDEAS FOR MODERN WEAR
JOHN MARSHALL

Kodansha
International
Ltd.

TOKYO & NEW YORK

To Mary Tsukamoto,
with deepest respect, love,
and gratitude

The title page decoration is a collection of traditional *hanten* jackets displaying the crests and symbols of various merchants and artisans.

Photographs of outer robe and all tabi socks except leather pair by Steven Jenner. All other photographs by Jeffrey Westman. Line drawings of garment pattern layouts by Mari Lee. All other drawings by the author.

Book design by
Seventeenth Street Studios.
Type composition by
Another Point, Inc.

Distributed in the United States by Kodansha International/USA Ltd., through Harper & Row, Publishers, Inc., 10 East 53rd Street, New York, New York 10022.

Published by Kodansha International Ltd., 2-2, Otowa 1-chome, Bunkyo-ku, Tokyo 112 and Kodansha International/USA Ltd., 10 East 53rd Street, New York, New York 10022.

Library of Congress Cataloging-in-Publication Data
Marshall, John, 1955–
  Make your own Japanese clothes.
  Bibliography: p.
  Includes index.
  1. Clothing and dress. 2. Costume—Japan. I. Title.
TT507.M366   1988   646'.47   87-82861
ISBN 0-87011-865-X (U.S.)
ISBN 4-7700-1365-5 (Japan)

Contents

color photographs on pages 59–66

Symbols Used in This Book

fold line

sewing line

cutting line
(on pattern layouts)

blindstitched fabric edge

all seam allowances are ½″
(unless otherwise specified)

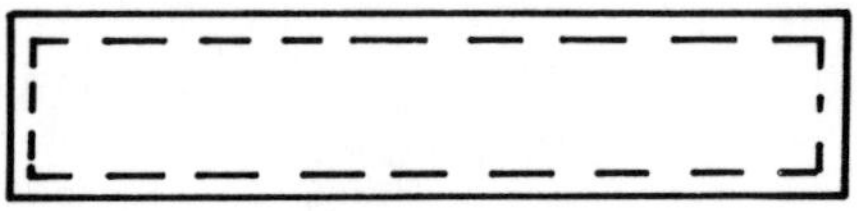

hollow arrow indicates placement behind fabric layer

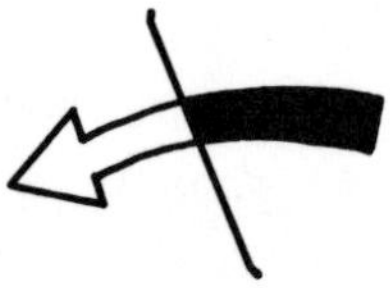

Introduction

One of the earliest human expressions of self through art came through decorating the body. From a humble beginning of simple patterns painted in mud on bare skin, evolved, through the centuries, more elaborate adornments such as jewelry and clothing.

While virtually all cultures developed garments of some sort, nomadic hunting cultures, who relied on relatively stiff, irregularly shaped animal hides for materials, developed complex patterns and form-fitting garment shapes.

On the other hand, agrarian cultures, who had access to steady sources of plant and animal fiber, designed simpler patterns with straighter lines and garment shapes dependent on tucking and draping in order to avoid cutting into their labor-intensive fabrics.

Japan was one such agrarian culture, whose strong weaving tradition formed the basis of kimono design. All traditional Japanese garments are styled for minimal cutting or waste of the fabric while achieving sophisticated and graceful lines.

The width of fabric produced in Japan has varied substantially over the course of history, but modern-day fabric for sewing traditional clothing is a fairly standard 14½″ wide. "Double-width" (29″) and "triple-width" (43″) fabric in traditional fibers and weaves are also available in Japan, but less commonly so.

The narrow width of Japanese fabric necessitates a center back seam in all garments (except those for children) as well as a front opening. That is, two strips of narrow fabric are joined along half of their length to form the back of the garment and the other ends of the strips are brought over the shoulders to form the front panels.

Nearly all cuts into Japanese fabric are made from selvedge to selvedge along the weft threads. Even when a pattern piece would be too wide, the Japanese avoid cutting along the lengthwise grain (the warp), which would weaken the integrity of the weave. The preference in traditional sewing is to take larger seam allowances.

The rectangular pattern pieces are assembled, a few tucks and easements added, and the garment is complete. Children's garments have additional tucks made at the shoulders and waist after the garment is sewn. The garment can then be let out as the wearer grows.

Because the silhouette has remained relatively uncluttered, great emphasis has been placed on surface design throughout Japan's history of costume. Many styles of weaving, dyeing, and stitchery have reached their peak in Japan,

Introduction

resulting in some of the most exquisite textiles the world has known.

Certainly it is the fabric—its beautiful colors, exotic motifs, and quality of weave—that first attracted Westerners to Japanese garments. The most sought-after of these textiles is silk, as this was the fiber favored by the aristocrats and the wealthy and thus the object of elaborate technical artistry. Indeed, silk is recommended for many of the patterns in this book.

Today many Western textile artists continue to draw inspiration from Japanese fabrics, exploring traditional as well as innovative surface design techniques. It is no longer unusual to see knit kimono or leather *hanten* jackets in fine art-to-wear boutiques in major U.S. cities.

Another appeal of traditional Japanese clothing is the fit. Most garments are designed to drape loosely and are closed with ties whose tightness is adjustable. Although properly donned women's kimono may seem restricting to the novice, with modifications in the style of wear, they can be very comfortable. Suggestions for innovative wear are made throughout this book.

Versatility is yet another attraction of Japanese clothes. Japanese work clothes, such as the *hanten* jacket, and kimono overgarments, such as the *haori* jacket, can easily be worn in conjunction with Western clothes. The simple yet elegant lines of Japanese garments make them a suitable, stylish choice for work and play.

Over the last hundred years kimono have fallen increasingly into disuse in Japan. As lifestyles become busier, there is less time to spend on dressing and caring for clothes. Chairs, cars, and other elements introduced from the West are simply not conducive to kimono wear.

As a result, kimono are now rarely worn outside of formal occasions in Japan—weddings, Coming-of-Age ceremonies (at age twenty), and funerals—or classes in traditional arts, such as tea ceremony, flower arranging, music, and dance.

On the other hand, simple cotton *yukata* (summer kimono) are still the favorite for lounging at summer resorts and hot springs, and all of the other informal garments presented in this book have enthusiastic followings in Japan, whether among gardeners and farmers, festival performers and shopkeepers, or students and housewives.

For the kimono to survive, it must continue to evolve, as it has over the centuries, to meet the changing needs of modern society. Westerners have already played a role in this development, by borrowing from the Japanese clothing tradition and using its simple lines and drape as a foundation for innovative expression in fashion and art.

Take this book and use it as a creative resource. The traditional methods and patterns have been altered slightly in some cases to better suit Western needs and lifestyles, but feel free to develop them further.

In this manner kimono will continue to evolve and thrive in their new identity as practical, attractive, comfortable clothing for both East and West.

PART ONE

Before You Begin

1 Japanese Tools and Stitches

Sewing traditional clothing—kimono, in particular—is an exacting art in Japan. Collars, sleeves, and hems must drape just so; the stitching must be easily removable for washing the garment piece by piece; the entire garment, in fact, must be sewn by hand to achieve the ideal results. These results include proper fit and protection of the fabric (handstitching will rip before the fabric does when a seam undergoes stress). Accordingly, you will not find racks of readymade quality kimono in department stores. Rather, department stores, as well as neighborhood *gofukuya*, or tailor shops, sell bolts of narrow fabric and sew each kimono by hand to order. Times do change, however. Recently, readymade one-size-fits-all kimono of lined polyester have made their debut, while inexpensive cotton summer kimono (*yukata*) have been mass-produced for some time.

For wear in the West, Japanese clothes need not be constructed in the time-honored, and often quite time-consuming, traditional ways. A kimono is bound to receive heavier wear as a party dress or dressing gown than as the garb of choice for studying the sedate tea ceremony. Accordingly, it might make more sense, for example, to make a kimono from a more easily washable fabric than silk and to use a sewing machine where possible.

Whether to use traditional sewing techniques and tools—like all choices made when sewing—is a function of such factors as the purpose of the garment (to wear seldom or many times, to wear to a party or while gardening), the end wearer (a meticulous wardrobe caretaker or a "permanent-press only" dresser), the time available to devote to construction, and so on. Only you can weigh the factors and make the appropriate choices.

Described in this chapter are basic traditional Japanese sewing tools and handstitching techniques, both of which may be employed in non-Japanese sewing projects as well. The tools are illustrated and described in detail to help you in improvising substitutes. See Appendix 2 for tool suppliers. Many of the stitches will appear familiar and are indeed universally used.

JAPANESE TOOLS

Thimbles

The Japanese thimble (*yubinuki*), shaped much like a cigar band, is designed to fit around the first joint of the middle finger (Fig. 1.1). Hold

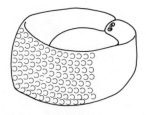

1.1. Japanese thimble

the needle between the index finger and thumb with the blunt (eye) end of the needle constantly resting against the thimble (Fig. 1.2). Use the thimble to push the needle through the fabric as the fingers guide the needle on its course.

Japanese thimbles are made of leather, metal, or plastic. Some people even make their own of fabric-encased cardboard. Leather is the most comfortable and practical material. Plastic and metal thimbles are usually wider and therefore don't fit as well. In addition, their hard surfaces tend to cause the needle to slip and the thread to break as it is ground between needle and thimble.

Clippers

Japanese scissors (*nippon-basami*) do not have blades joined at a pivotal point as do Western scissors. Instead the blades are fashioned from a single piece of metal that is bent in the middle to give the clippers a springlike action (Fig. 1.3). They can be very handy when it comes to quick clips of thread and cloth. Be sure to grip them well behind the blades to prevent cutting your fingers. For maximum convenience, keep a pair tied to your sewing machine with a ribbon so they will always be at the ready. In former times, larger versions of these clippers were used to cut out patterns, but in modern times Western-style scissors are the standard tool of choice for extensive cutting of fabric.

Iron

The Japanese iron (*denki-gote*) has a long tail-like handle and is a bit squatter than Western irons (Fig. 1.4). It is well designed for fitting into confined areas, such as the lower inside corners of kimono sleeves. Japanese irons range in size from 3″ to 10″ long. A small (Western) travel iron makes an adequate substitute.

Marking Stylus

Made of ivory, horn, or plastic, the Japanese marking stylus (*hera*) is used in place of tailor's chalk to score marks on cloth (Fig. 1.5). Grasp the stylus firmly by the handle and pull it toward you while pressing down. The rounded drawing edge is somewhat sharp and may damage delicate fabrics. For this reason, it is better to place fabric to be scored on a Japanese cutting board than to score fabric directly on a hard surface like a tabletop. Dull letter openers make good substitutes or you can fashion your own stylus by cutting a plastic ruler to the shape illustrated. File the rounded scoring edge to a blunt point and sand all edges smooth.

Cutting Board

In a Japanese home a cutting board (*tachi-ita*) is laid out when working on tatami floors to protect the matting (Fig. 1.6). The board consists of a thick Bristol board core covered on one side with sturdy handmade paper or woven cotton. Sewing reminders, standard kimono measurements, conversion charts, and graph lines are printed on the reverse side. The board, 16″ × 66″ when spread out, folds up accordion-style to about the size of a large book for easy storage.

1.2. Using a Japanese thimble

1.3. Japanese clippers

1.4. Japanese iron

1.5. Marking stylus

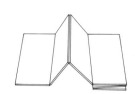
1.6. Japanese cutting board

This is the best type of board to use with the marking stylus. It has some give to it, unlike most tabletops, yet not as much give as a carpeted floor, which would allow the stylus to cut through the cloth or distort the weave. Similar cutting boards, calibrated with both metric and inch measurements, are available in American sewing stores; a typical board is made of cardboard and measures 40″ × 72″.

"Third Hand"

The "third hand" (*kakehari*) is a truly wonderful device (Fig. 1.7). You will find it quite useful when doing any handsewing. Currently it is marketed in the United States under the name Third Hand and is made of aluminum to a length of about 3½″. In earlier times, it was referred to as an "Elizabethan nightingale" because of its birdlike shape.

The back end (tail) is attached by a cord to an immovable object, such as the sewing box mentioned below. The front end (beak) has two small rubber grips that open when the center sections (wings) are pushed together. When the wings are released, the beak clamps down on the fabric and the rubber pads keep it from pulling loose. Thus, with the fabric secured, one hand is totally freed to do the stitching; in essence, you are indeed working with a third hand. The clamp is moved along as the sewing progresses. The other end of the cord may be tied to a safety pin, and the pin attached to a sofa arm in lieu of the sewing box. You may also find it convenient to pin it to your pant leg when wearing jeans. That way your leg may

be used as well to adjust the tension of the fabric.

Sleeve Template

A template of cardboard or plastic may be used as a guide when marking the curve on the front lower corner of each sleeve. Using a sleeve template insures that the sleeves on a garment will have uniform sizes and curves. You can use a French curve to make a template with four corner variations (Fig. 1.8). Or, place saucers, cups, or jars upside down on the cardboard and trace to make the different curves.

Sewing Box

The Japanese sewing box (*haribako*) is certainly not necessary for creating beautiful garments, but it is a practical and attractive sewing accessory (Fig. 1.9). Its ingenious design includes a "foot" that attaches to the bottom, upon which one kneels to stabilize the base when using a "third hand." One end of the "third hand" is tied through a small hole in the neck. A measuring stick—calibrated in centimeters or in the traditional Japanese system of *sun* (inches) and *shaku* (feet)—slips into a slot built into the neck or body of the box. A pincushion is built into the top of the neck over a tiny drawer, and the entire wooden box is made easily portable by a handle attached to the top.

1.7. "Third hand"

1.8. Using a French curve to make a sleeve template

1.9. Japanese sewing box

JAPANESE HANDSTITCHING

All you really need to handsew is needle and thread. Japanese needles are virtually identical to those made in the West, so use whatever stainless steel needles you have on hand, selecting one appropriate to the weight of the fabric. Silk thread is preferred for handsewing, especially when using silk fabric. Not only is silk thread strong and resilient, but it glides smoothly through the weave during sewing and is easy to remove when necessary. You may substitute more readily available thread, such as cotton-covered polyester.

Knotting the Thread

Before beginning to handsew, knot one end of the thread by wrapping the thread around your index finger and rolling it off between thumb and index finger while pulling it tight into a tiny ball. It helps to moisten the thread end first.

To finish off handsewing with a knot, lay the needle on top of the last stitch, wrap the remaining thread a few times around the needle, and pull the needle out while pinching the knot area between thumb and forefinger (Figs. 1.10, 1.11).

To finish off handsewing without making an actual knot, take a small backstitch (Fig. 1.12), then reverse direction and sew back over the line of stitching for an inch or so (Fig. 1.13). Tuck under the thread (Fig. 1.14), and trim off the excess. This type of finishing may be desirable to avoid a lumpy knot when sewing on fine fabrics or to enable easy disassembly of the garment for piece-by-piece washing.

Running Stitch

The running stitch (*naminui*) is used primarily to join seams. When Japanese sew a running stitch, they hold the needle still and move the fabric onto it. (See Figure 1.2 for a bird's-eye view of the correct way to hold the threaded needle.) Every few stitches the accumulated fabric is scooted off the needle.

Figures 1.15 and 1.16 show the proper way to gather fabric onto the needle. Hold the needle securely between the thumb and index finger of the right hand, with the "third hand" supporting the right edge of the fabric. The other three fingers of the right hand are used to scoot the stitched fabric off the needle in the direction of the "third hand." With the left hand, hold the fabric along the line to be stitched, pulling gently against the resistance of the "third hand." Insert the needle in the fabric and, with the left hand, pull the fabric up (and onto the needle) and down (and onto the needle) in alternation. Periodically check and, if necessary, even out the tension of the stitched thread. The thread should not cause any puckering in the fabric.

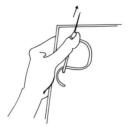

1.11

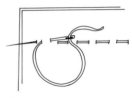

1.12

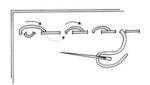

1.13

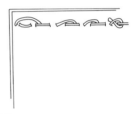

1.14

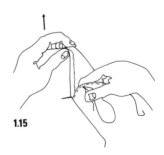

1.15

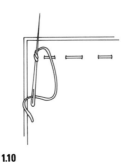

1.10

1.16

Reinforcement Stitch

Use a reinforcement stitch (*kannuki-dome*) to help relieve strain on fabric and thread where the sleeve joins the body of the garment at the underarm opening. This stitch is used on the front and back of women's kimono sleeves. You might also use it to reinforce the side seams of slacks having a tie closing.

First, stitch twice across the seam where the sleeve joins the body (Fig. 1.17). Then wrap the double-stranded loop with tight half hitches (Fig. 1.18) until the loop is full. Tie off (Fig. 1.19) and clip the thread end. For extra strength, pass the needle through the middle of the loop to the starting point and then clip the thread.

Parallel Stitching

Use parallel stitching (*nido-nui*)—two parallel rows of running stitches—for the center back seam of a garment that consists of selvedge edges or a fold of fabric. (For raw edges, finish with a French seam.) This seam receives more stress than most, so the second line of stitching serves as a backup in case the first line of stitching pulls out.

Stitch the first line with a ⅛″ seam allowance and the second line with a ½″ seam allowance or whatever seam allowance is appropriate to size the garment (Fig. 1.20).

French Seams

Make French seams (*fukuro-nui*) when joining cut fabric edges, such as the bottom edges of the sleeves, in an unlined garment. With wrong sides together, sew along the fabric edges leaving a ⅛″

seam allowance. Reverse the seam so right sides of fabric are together and sew along the regular seam allowance (Fig. 1.21).

Backstitch

Use a backstitch (*hangaeshi-nui*) to join seams that will be subject to a lot of pull and stretch. This stitch helps relieve tension that may cause the thread to break, while keeping the fabric in proper alignment. The example illustrated (Fig. 1.22) shows ⅛″ increments but any size stitch that does the job may be substituted. Insert the needle in the fabric, bringing it out ¼″ beyond. Backtrack ⅛″ and sew forward ⅜″. Backtrack ⅛″ and sew forward ⅜″. Repeat this pattern for the length of the seam.

1.19

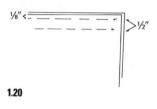

1.20

$⅛″$ `< ----------- >` $½″$

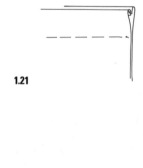

1.21

1.17

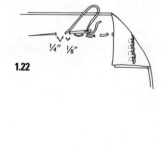

1.22

¼″ ⅛″

1.18

Holding Stitch

This loose stitch (*osae-nui*) is a relative of staystitching. Use it to hold the side seam allowance of a kimono flat to one side of the seam (Fig. 1.23), in which case it resembles a blindstitch. Or, to preserve the soft fold of a collar where it meets the garment body (Fig. 1.24), baste large (at least 1″) stitches ⅛″ from the seam line. This is also the stitch used to keep sleeve edges, hems, and some collars in place during long-term storage of a garment.

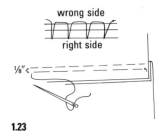

1.23

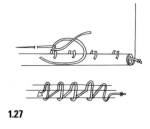

1.27

Blindstitch

Use a blindstitch when you desire no or minimal stitching to show on the right side of the garment. Blindstitches go by different names in Japanese depending on their function. Use *hashibuse-nui* (Fig. 1.25) to finish off a selvedge edge. Use *matsuri-guke* (Fig. 1.26) to finish off the raw edges of a partial lining. Use *yori-guke* (Fig. 1.27) to finish off the edges of unlined sleeve openings and the fore-edge of the overlaps on an unlined kimono. All types of blindstitch are represented by the same symbol (see p. vi) in this book.

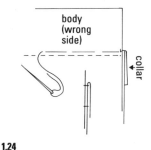

1.24

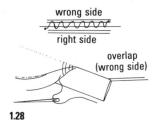

1.28

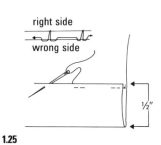

1.25

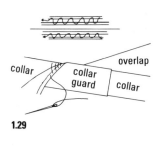

1.29

Slipstitch

Use a slipstitch (*hon-guke*) to stitch the back side of the collar in place (Fig. 1.28); to invisibly sew all edges of a collar guard (Fig. 1.29); or to construct tube ties (Fig. 1.30).

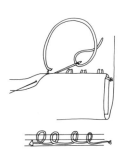

1.26

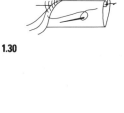

1.30

2 Making the Pattern

型どり

The kimono is designed to fit a Japanese ideal of the human body. This ideal has changed over time much as Western fashion has changed over the years to reflect changing views of the perfect figure.

Women's kimono are geared toward a contourless body. Many Japanese women have hour-glass figures and so find it necessary to pad out their waist and the hollow of their back to create a very uniform (cylindrical) appearance. Large-busted women in Japan wear undergarments that help to flatten the breasts and create a more even and graceful slope from the shoulders.

Men's kimono are geared to the same general contourless shape as well. Slightly squared shoulders, a long torso, and small shapeless hips are ideal for wearing a man's kimono. Having a paunch helps to keep a man's obi in place around the hips and enhances the overall look.

In Japan there is less variation in body sizes and shapes in the general population when compared to the United States with its diverse ethnic components. The proportions presented in this book are based on traditional Japanese proportions and the traditional look.

Carefully take your own body measurements (or those of the person you're sewing for), as outlined below. If you take all the measurements, you will be ready to make any of the garments in the book. Or, you can take only those measurements necessary for the garment you have selected.

Then, using your measurements, draw the pattern as explained below. Adjust the pattern with a trial fitting of the pattern pieces. Before drafting your pattern, be sure to read the tailoring tips, as these are the methods for altering the traditional fit to one potentially more suitable to your specific body type.

Suggestions for modifying the basic construction or look in more dramatic ways are provided as variations at the end of each garment's instructions. These variations are a further source of ideas for adapting kimono designs to Western ways of life. The possibilities are endless, so feel free to mix and match the basic garment elements to create your own daring new look.

TAKING YOUR BODY MEASUREMENTS

Photocopy Figures 2.1–5. You may want to enlarge Figures 2.1 and 2.2 to make room for notes. Take your measurements beginning with A below, and fill in the figures

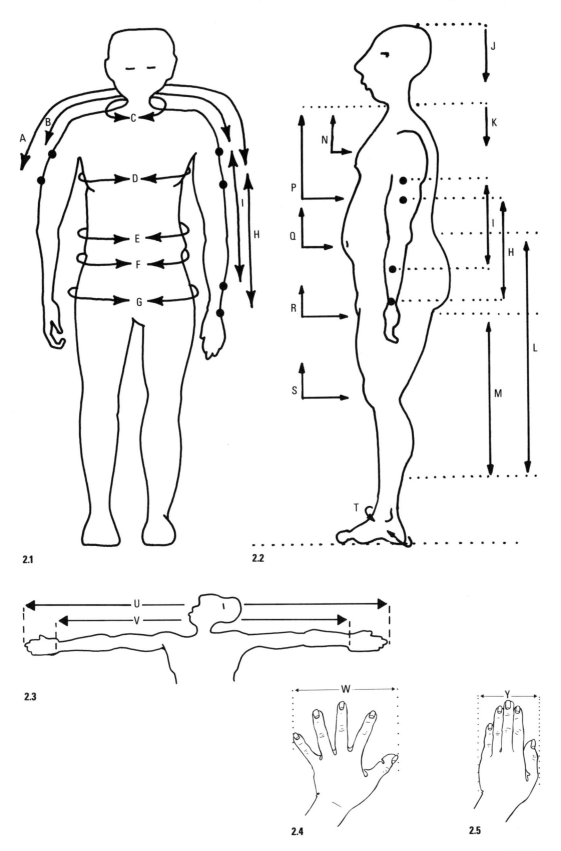

2.1

2.2

2.3

2.4

2.5

next to the corresponding letters on the photocopied sheets. (Letters O and X have been skipped to avoid confusion with mathematical symbols.) The aid of a friend will speed the process.

A. The distance from a point halfway between a woman's shoulder and elbow, across the back of her neck, to the corresponding point on her other arm. Measure while arms are hanging at sides. (This is the traditional length of a woman's kimono shoulder line.)

B. The distance from a point one-third of the way between a man's shoulder and elbow, across the back of his neck, to the corresponding point on his other arm. Measure while arms are hanging at sides. (This is the traditional length of a man's kimono shoulder line. It is also the recommended shoulder line for traditional work clothes for both sexes.)

C. The circumference of the base of the neck.

D. The circumference of the chest at its fullest point.

E. The circumference of the abdomen at the waist.

F. The circumference of the abdomen at its fullest point (for those people who have a protruding belly).

G. The circumference of the hips at their fullest point.

H. The distance from a woman's shoulder seam (see A) to her wrist when her arm is held at the side. (This is the traditional length of a woman's sleeve.)

I. The distance from a man's shoulder seam (see B) to a point two-thirds of the way down from his elbow to his wrist, when his arm is held at the side. (This is the traditional length of a man's sleeve.)

J. Height in stocking feet.

K. The distance from the base of the neck (the neck bone) to the floor.

L. The distance from the waist to the bottom of the calf muscle.

M. The distance from the crotch to the bottom of the calf muscle.

N. The distance from the top of the shoulder at the neck to mid-sternum.

P. The distance from the top of the shoulder at the neck to the base of the rib cage.

Q. The distance from the top of the shoulder at the neck to the navel.

R. The distance from the top of the shoulder at the neck to the base (cup) of the buttocks (or to the crotch).

S. The distance from the top of the shoulder at the neck to the bottom of the kneecap.

T. The circumference of the foot at the widest point measuring from the heel around the top of the foot.

U. The distance from fingertip to fingertip when the arms are outstretched. (Used for women's garments.)

V. The distance from wristbone to wristbone when the arms are outstretched. (Used for men's garments.)

W. The distance from the tip of the pinky finger to the tip of the thumb when the fingers are spread gently as wide as they will go.

Y. The width of the hand when closed.

DRAWING
THE PATTERN

Before buying any fabric read carefully through the instructions for the garment you intend to sew and study the pattern layout. Next, using your body measurements as a guide, redraw the pattern layout on graph paper. Plot your pattern so that one square of graph paper equals 1″. This will make it easier to enlarge the pattern later. Don't be surprised if the pattern pieces in your graph drawing appear a bit longer or wider than the original—proportions will differ with different body sizes.

All pattern layouts in this book have been plotted using 36″ width fabric, as this is the narrowest fabric in common use in the United States. You may, of course, use any width of fabric and rearrange the pattern pieces to suit your needs.

The easiest and surest way to determine how much fabric you are actually going to need is simply to cut out all your pattern pieces from pattern tracing cloth and lay them out on the floor or a table, being careful not to exceed the width of the fabric to be used. Measure the running length of these pieces and you have the yardage requirement. Be sure to allow extra if you are going to cut fabric with large patterns or one-way patterns that need to be matched. Always lay out the major pattern pieces so they line up with the straight of the grain. This will help ensure that the finished garment hangs properly. Very rarely is a Japanese pattern piece cut on the bias.

Fabric suggestions have been made under each garment heading, but feel free to use any fabric that strikes your fancy. If you plan to use a fabric that has a nap or grain, such as corduroy or velvet, you may want to add a seam at the shoulders so the nap runs in the same direction on front and back.

Figure 2.6 shows a typical pattern layout on traditional Japanese fabric, which is normally 13½″–15″ wide. Japanese frequently use fabric with a one-way pattern. With a traditional narrow-width pattern layout, this causes a portion of the design on the finished kimono to be upside down (Fig. 2.7). By Japanese standards this is fine, but follow your own tastes.

One solution to this comes in the fabric-dyeing stage. The fabric is designed with a repeating pattern in which every other element is upside down. In effect, some portion of the pattern in the finished kimono is always right-side up (Fig. 2.8). The Japanese consider this preferable to putting in a seam at the shoulder to right the pattern.

A number of readily available tools will help you draw the patterns in this book. The following are particularly handy:

Graph paper: Use graph paper for drawing a draft of your pattern in miniature. A paper with a large grid broken into units of twelve is easiest for plotting in inches. Grids subdivided into units of ten work best with the metric system.

Pattern tracing cloth: Two materials suitable for pattern pieces are available at well-stocked sewing stores. One, called "pattern tracing cloth," is a lightweight synthetic fabric covered with a grid of dots spaced 1″ apart; it resembles

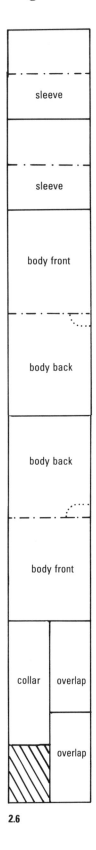

2.6

interfacing in texture. The other, "pattern paper," resembles butcher paper in texture and also has a 1″ dot grid. Grids greatly facilitate the transferral of the graph paper pattern. These materials come in widths of 36″ or 45″.

Felt-tip pen: Use a broad-tip indelible marking pen to transfer your original graph paper drawing to the pattern tracing cloth. It's a good idea to place newspaper under the cloth when drawing. Different colors may be used to distinguish different bits of information, such as cutting lines, fold lines, and pattern piece labels.

Yardstick: Use a yardstick when drawing your pattern to help keep the lines straight.

Large envelopes: Large manilla envelopes are ideal for sorting and storing your pattern pieces once they have been drafted and cut out.

Calculator: Use of a pocket calculator may speed the pattern-drafting process, as many of the dimensions are based on proportions and formulas.

Masking tape: Straight pins and masking tape are useful in attaching the pattern pieces together for a quick trial wearing before actually cutting the cloth.

Before beginning to stitch together a garment, carefully iron the fabric, taking care to press out any natural stretch in the weave. This is advisable even if the fabric has been preshrunk. (Preshrinking and ironing all fabric before cutting out the pattern pieces is a good idea.) If a flat weave stretches after the garment is completed, the result will be unattractive baggy areas at the knees and seat.

TRIAL FITTING

Transfer the graph-paper pattern to the pattern tracing cloth, enlarging to life-size proportions. Cut out the pieces. Tape, or pin, all pieces together as though you were sewing the garment together. Try the garment on. If the fit is off, first doublecheck the measurements and calculations. Make sure you have taken proper seam allowances, made all appropriate tucks, and so on. Does it fit well? Are the sleeves the proper length? Is it the look you envisioned? Or is it too loose or too snug in some areas? Now is the time to make any design changes. (See Tailoring Tips below for extra help.)

To alter your pattern pieces first unpin (or untape) the area to be altered. If the garment is too large in that area, trim off some of the tracing fabric until you achieve the proper fit. If the pattern is too small, or if you inadvertently cut off too much while altering it, add pieces of scrap pattern tracing cloth with masking tape. When adding pieces, keep the printed grid lined up properly.

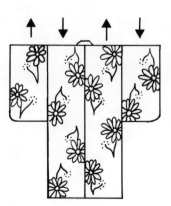

2.7

2.8

TAILORING TIPS

These guidelines will help you achieve the proper fit. Read each one and, where appropriate, incorporate the suggestions when drafting your pattern.

Measuring Your Neck

Construction of a neck opening template is necessary to ensure proper fit of a collar around the neck. All garments with a neck opening require these measurements.

1. Divide C (the circumference of the base of your neck) by 4. On a piece of paper draw a perfect square using this figure for each side (Fig. 2.9).

2. Divide C by 8. Extend the bottom side of the square by this figure on each side (Fig. 2.10). This base line will align with the garment's shoulder line.

3. Draw curved lines from the base line to the top corners of the square (Fig. 2.11).

4. Transfer the neck-line shape to a piece of cardboard and mark the center of the top and bottom edges. Cut it out and write your name and the date on it. Your neck opening template is ready to trace onto the fabric.

5. To transfer the neck opening shape to the fabric, line up the bottom of the neck opening template with the garment shoulder line and trace the curved edge with tailor's chalk or a marking stylus. Extend the lines to the bottom hem line of the garment front (Fig. 2.12). This inverted U shape is the collar sewing line.

Tailoring Jackets

According to the Japanese aesthetic, the shoulder–sleeve seam on a woman's garment should hit halfway between the shoulder and elbow (Fig. 2.13). On men the ideal shoulder line falls one-third of the way down from the shoulder to the elbow (Fig. 2.14).

2.9

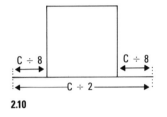

2.10

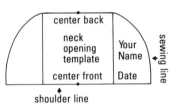

2.11

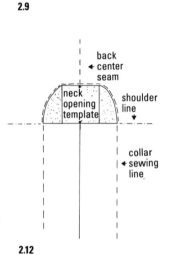

2.12

2.13

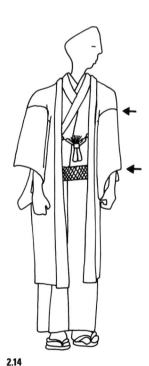

2.14

Making the Pattern

One reason for these proportions is to provide extra yardage around the body.

If you prefer a more Western fit—that is, a slimmer, less voluminous fit around the torso—in a *hanten* or *haori* jacket, follow these easy steps:

1. Calculate a new shoulder line measurement: Take the largest of your measurements E, F, and G. We'll use G in the example. Add half of C and divide this sum by 2: $(G + \frac{1}{2}C) \div 2$. Use the result as your shoulder measurement in place of A (women) or B (men).

2. Calculate a new sleeve length: Deduct your new shoulder measurement from U (women) or V (men). Divide by 2 to derive the length of each sleeve. Thus, for women, $(U - \text{new shoulder line measurement}) \div 2 = \text{new sleeve length}$. For men, $(V - \text{new shoulder line measurement}) \div 2 = \text{new sleeve length}$. See Figure 2.15.

Tailoring Full-Length Garments

Torso proportions vary widely from person to person. To achieve a more tailored fit on a shapely figure (one with variation among chest, waist, and hip measurements), you may want to taper the sides of the kimono or outer robe body instead of keeping the traditional straight lines.

First, take the largest of your measurements E, F, and G. (We'll use G in the example.) Add half of measurement C. Divide the sum by 2. In other words, calculate $(G + \frac{1}{2}C) \div 2$. Which is larger, the result or measurement A (B for men)?

If A (B) is larger by 3″ or more, draw the body pattern piece as shown in Figure 2.16. Plot A (B) at the shoulder line. Draw a parallel line a distance of P from the shoulder line. Plot and center the above calculation—$(G + \frac{1}{2}C) \div 2$—on the parallel line. Connect the shoulder line to these points, and continue straight down to the hem line.

If A (B) is within 2″–3″ of the result, follow Figure 2.17 (the same as the traditional proportions presented in the patterns).

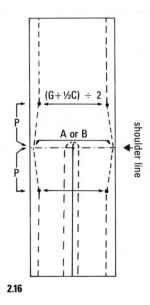

2.16

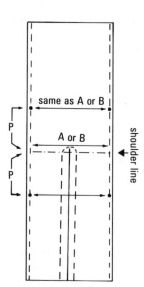

2.17

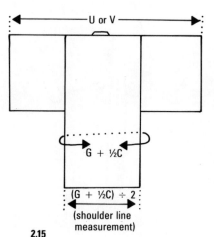

2.15

If A (B) is smaller by 3″ or more, draw the body pattern piece as shown in Figure 2.18. If sewn on without adjustment (Fig. 2.19), the sleeves could cause excessive bunching when the arms are held at the sides. To prevent this, you may wish to widen the top of the sleeve and shorten the shoulder line as shown in Figure 2.20. This nontraditional alteration also causes the shoulder seam to fall a bit higher on the arm than normal, but the garment will fit more comfortably.

Fitting the Bustline

If your bust at its fullest point (D) is the largest of your torso measurements, you may find that the garment binds under the arms. The best two ways to prevent this from happening are to make wrapped sleeves (*makisode*) or to widen the armholes when attaching other sleeves.

For large-breasted women, the most comfortable garment in this book is *Hanten* Jacket Variation 3 (p. 81). This type of sleeve is widest at the point where it hits the body; the bottom of the sleeve extends to the waist or below. The result is a great deal of fullness in the upper area of the garment and elimination of binding under the arms.

Even if you select a different pattern, use the *hanten* jacket variation as a key: Design your garment to have sleeves that hit lower than is otherwise indicated. For *hanten* jackets, *jimbei* tops, and *hippari* tops, this simply means fuller, wider sleeves. For *haori* jackets, make the gusset wider at the top as well. For kimono and outer robes, attach more of the sleeve to the body and extend

the small opening in the side seam under the sleeve. (In this case, you will have to wear your obi a bit lower than normal.) The priority in making these alterations is comfort.

ADDING A BACK SEAM

The pattern layouts in this book do not show a center back seam line, although allowance (1″) has been made for such a seam in the pattern dimensions. (Exceptions are the wraparound tops, which have a box pleat instead, and the vests.) The assumption is that most readers will use wider, Western-width fabrics, eliminating the need for a cut line (seam) in the body back.

While the center back seam may be omitted without affecting the garment structure, from the Japanese point of view it is considered an important design element as well as a protection against misfortune (see box).

To add a back seam, simply fold the body back in half, right sides facing, and sew together ½″ from the folded edge. Repeat for lining and polyfil batting, if applicable.

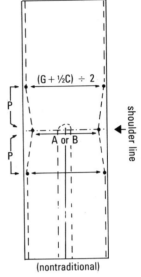

(G + ½C) ÷ 2

shoulder line

A or B

(nontraditional)

2.18

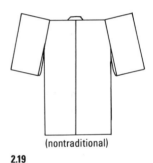

(nontraditional)

2.19

U or V

(G + ½C) ÷ 2

(nontraditional)

2.20

GARMENT CHARMS

Semori (literally, "back protectors") are motifs stitched on garments to protect the wearers from evil influences. These charms are placed high on the back of the garment, just between the shoulder blades. *Semori* are most often seen on children's garments and on adults' garments having no center back seam, the belief being that a center back seam serves the same function as a charm.

Garment charms come in a variety of forms, the most common of which are stitched or embroidered in thread that contrasts attractively with the colors of the garment. Some examples of typical designs are shown here. More elaborate embroidery as well as appliqué and miniature cloth dolls may also be incorporated into charm designs.

Stitch on the charm with embroidery thread when the garment is complete. When the charm becomes worn or faded, remove the thread and embroider a new charm.

Packet of paper strips
(*tabane-noshi*)

Three arrow feathers (*mitsuya*)

Oarsman (*funahiki*)

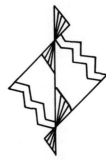

Double fans (*chigai ogi*)

Crane (*tsuru*)

Pine needles (*matsuba*)

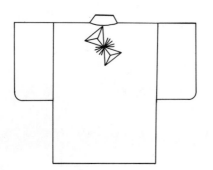

Pine boughs (*matsu*)

Paper butterfly (*noshicho*)

PART TWO

The Basic Elements

3 Padding

綿入れ

Hanten jackets, vests, and kimono are padded for extra warmth in winter. Presented here are two methods for padding a garment. The first is the traditional method wherein there is little or no stitching through the layers to hold the batting in place. The secret to this method is the use of *mawata*, or an expanded silk cocoon, between the face fabric and the batting. *Mawata* is available at Japanese sewing supplies shops but difficult to find in the United States (old-fashioned variety stores in Japanese communities are one potential source). Store-bought *mawata* is pure white and resembles a folding military cap in shape and size (Fig. 3.3).

The second method for padding a garment is not traditional, but it is better suited for machine sewing and synthetic batting materials. It is the method recommended throughout the book.

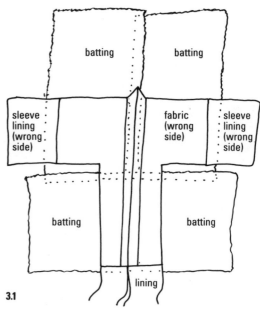

3.1

TRADITIONAL METHOD

For this method, you need 6–10 *mawata* (silk cocoons) and sufficient wool or cotton batting to cover the entire garment except for the collar. Although wool is more expensive, it is lighter in weight and

tends not to mat together as much as cotton when washed. If synthetic batting is substituted, the polyfil method outlined below will yield more satisfactory results.

Before you begin the padding process, the garment should be nearly complete: All face fabric pieces should be sewn together, and the collar should be sewn along one edge to the face fabric. The lining should be at the stage shown in Figure 4.7.

Plan to work on a large smooth surface, such as a dining room table or hardwood floor. Because of the fineness of the cocoon silk, it feels almost sticky and tends to cling to nearly everything it touches.

3.2

3.3

1. Lay the batting out on a flat surface so that when the garment is (later) laid on top, the batting will fold over to cover the whole garment. Depending on the width of the batting, you may have to overlap in places, as shown in Figure 3.1.

2. Feather all overlapping edges to reduce bulk. To feather, pull gently on cut edges, removing about ½″ of batting as you go (Fig. 3.2).

3. Prepare each silk cocoon (Fig. 3.3) by slitting one side to the center (Fig. 3.4).

4. Grasp the two flaps formed and carefully pull out (Fig. 3.5) into a fine gossamer web. Lay the web on the reverse side of the face fabric. Cover the wrong side of all fabric pieces except the collar (Fig. 3.6).

5. Lay the garment, cocoon side out, on top of the batting as shown in Figure 3.1. Fold the batting around to the front (Figs. 3.7, 3.8). Feather all overlapping edges.

6. Use a piece of cording to give the hem a clean line and add a bit of weight: Twist a 5″ wide strip of batting (long enough to go around the hem), evening out the thickness as you go (Fig. 3.9). When finished, grasp the ends and give it a gentle pull to compact the batting somewhat. Lay this cording on the batting at the hem line with enough batting below to form a casing when the lining is brought up (Fig. 3.10). Feather the edge of the batting to prevent bulkiness from echoing through the fabric. (This cording step is optional.)

7. If *mawata* is difficult to obtain or very expensive in your region, you may opt to cover only the wrong side of the face fabric with the

cocoon silk and later (step 9) lightly baste the seams of the lining to the batting. Otherwise, now is the time to cover the lining body and sleeves with a layer of silk web.

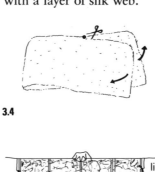

3.4

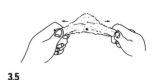

3.5

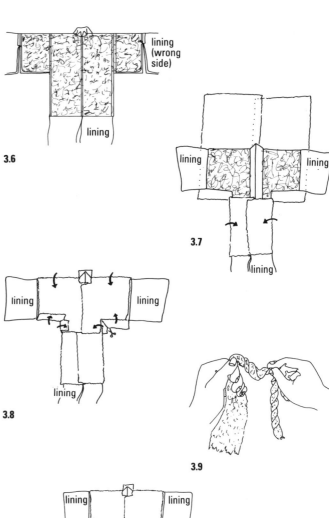

3.6

3.7

3.8

3.9

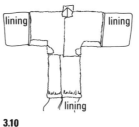

3.10

8. Gently pull the body lining up into position and fold the sleeve linings over the padded sleeves (Figs. 3.11, 3.12).

9. Whether or not you laid *mawata* on the lining, it is a good idea to baste the lining to the batting to keep the garment from ballooning. Sew within the seam allowance about ⅛″ from the seam line, catching only the batting and lining layers (Fig. 3.13). Baste back seam, side seams, and overlap seam (if there is one) in this manner.

10. Add a small scrap of batting (about 3″ square) to the bottom front corners for extra body (Fig. 3.13).

11. Fold the face fabric over the batting, between the bottom of the collar and the hem, and sew it with a holding stitch through the batting to the front (Fig. 3.14).

12. With the raw edge of the lining folded under, pin the lining in place and blindstitch up from the hem to the bottom of the collar (Fig. 3.15).

13. Fold under the raw edges of the sleeve lining and body lining where they join, and blindstitch the seam closed (Fig. 3.16). Finish off the collar.

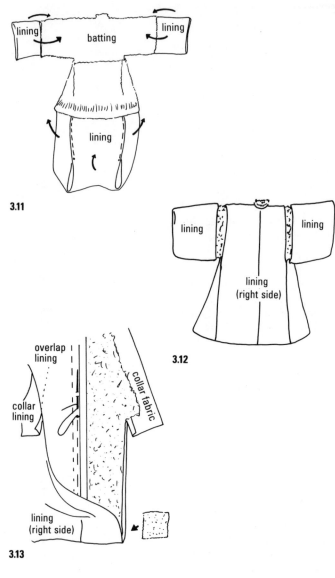

3.11

3.12

3.13

3.14

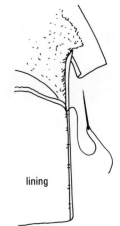

3.15

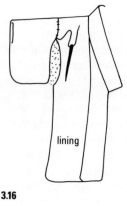

3.16

POLYFIL METHOD

This method was devised for use with a synthetic batting. As a general rule, a very soft batting with glazing on both sides works best. The glazing helps keep the batting fiber from working through the fabric.

1. Cut out batting pieces shown in the garment pattern layout. If no batting pattern is given, use the fabric pattern as a guide in cutting batting to fit each section to be padded (Fig. 3.17).

2. Feather all batting edges as shown in Figure 3.2.

3. Lay the wrong side of each face fabric piece on the corresponding batting piece and baste together with long running stitches within the ½" seam allowance (Fig. 3.18). From this point on, treat the fabric/batting piece as one unit. The batting side will be the equivalent of the "wrong side of the fabric." The layers will be stitched together more securely as the garment seams are machine-sewn together.

4. If you have trouble with the batting getting caught in the foot of your machine, or if the feed can't get enough traction to advance the batting properly, sandwich the fabric/batting piece between two pieces of tissue paper before sewing the garment together (Fig. 3.19). Stitch through all layers to join seams. Tear away the tissue after each seam is sewn.

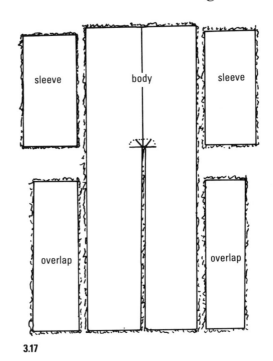

sleeve · body · sleeve

overlap · overlap

3.17

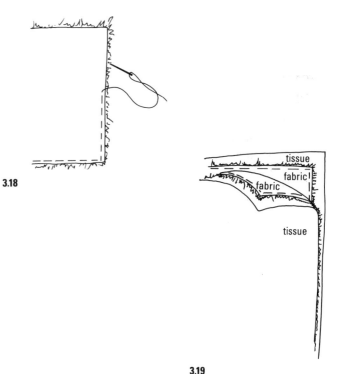

3.18

tissue

fabric

fabric

tissue

3.19

4 Linings

裏つけ

In Japan, garments are often categorized by whether they are lined or not. Lined garments are called *awase* and unlined garments *hitoe*. There are two types of linings: full and partial. Full linings provide extra warmth and strength and entirely cover the inside of the garment, eliminating the need for some of the finishing steps. Partial linings are used when full linings would be too bulky or too warm, such as in summer clothing.

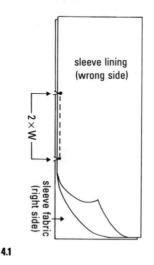

4.1

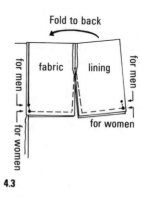

4.3

FULL LINING

When fully lining a garment, you need lining fabric for the body, sleeves, and sometimes even the collar. To determine the amount of yardage required, consult the lining pattern layout under the garment heading.

The order in which the lining pieces are assembled is not so important. One option is suggested here, but if a different order works better for you, by all means use it. The garment illustrated here is a "generic" garment designed to represent all garments. Details may differ (e.g., a kimono would have an overlap showing, the collar on a *hanten* jacket would extend the full

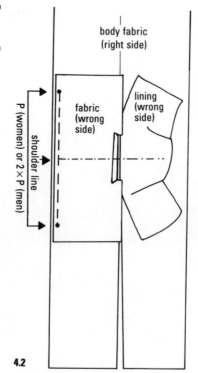

4.2

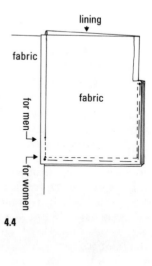

4.4

length of the front opening), but the principles apply for all.

1. Cut out all the lining pieces.

2. To line wrapped sleeves (*makisode*), see *Hanten* Jacket (p. 76). For all other sleeves, sew the lining to the sleeves along the wristhole (Fig. 4.1). Clip at dots. Press open seam.

3. Right sides together, attach fabric sleeve to fabric body (Fig. 4.2). Sew from shoulder line to each dot in turn. See Sleeves (Fig. 5.12) for position of dots.

4. Fold lining and fabric sleeves in half, right sides together (Fig. 4.3), and stitch between large points. Then arrange so lining is against sleeve back (Fig. 4.4). Baste through all layers between large points. This line will be curved for sleeves with rounded corners.

5. If your sleeves have a rounded corner, continue with steps 4 (starting with third sentence)–9 of Sleeves, treating the face and lining fabrics as one. When finished, your rounded sleeves should look like Figures 4.5 (inside out) and 4.6 (right-side out).

6. Return to the garment instructions to assemble the body. With right sides together, sew the body lining pieces together along side seams, center back seam, and (if applicable) overlap seams.

7. With right sides together, sew the body lining to the fabric along the bottom hem (Fig. 4.7).

8. Position the body lining and fabric so right sides are together. Note how on some hems the fabric curves around to the inside of the garment before meeting the lining (as shown here). Sew the front opening from the bottom of the garment to the point where the collar will begin (Fig. 4.8). Skip this step if the collar extends to the bottom of the hem, as in *hanten* jackets, *haori* jackets, and vests. Turn bottom hem edge of garment right-side out.

9. Pull sleeves through lining armholes as shown in Figures 4.9 and 4.10. The garment

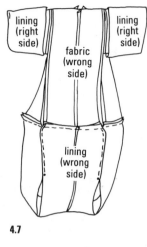

4.7

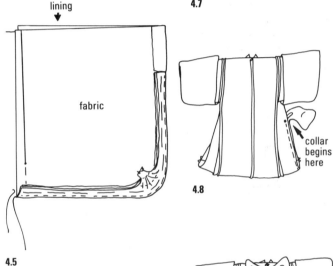

lining

fabric

4.5

fabric
(right side)

4.6

4.8

collar
begins
here

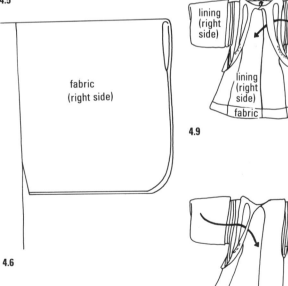

lining
(right
side)

lining
(right
side)

fabric

4.9

4.10

should resemble Figures 4.11 (back view) and 4.12 (front view). With right sides together, sew the lining sleeves to the lining body. Do this by reaching through the opening between lining and fabric at the collar line. On women's garments, finish by sewing the lining to the fabric around the sleeve back opening and side seam opening.

10. Turn the entire garment right-side out. Baste together all layers at the collar line (Fig. 4.13). Return to the garment instructions to complete. When the garment is finished, remove any basting that shows.

4.11

4.12

4.13

PARTIAL LINING

A partial lining is usually added in three areas: the sleeve openings, the shoulders, and the seat. The sleeve lining is actually more of a facing designed to add visual interest to the sleeve opening(s) as well as to absorb some of the wear. The shoulder and seat linings contribute to a graceful drape and more comfortable wear by reducing friction between undergarments and the garment's outer fabric. The seat lining also helps prevent the seat fabric from stretching out.

Sleeve Facings (Unlined Garment)

For sleeve facings, a lightweight, smooth fabric is normally used, often in a contrasting color, although the garment's face fabric is also a common choice. The sleeve facings are most easily attached before sewing any other sleeve seams.

1. Cut out two wristhole facings, one for each sleeve, as shown in Figure 4.14.

2. Fold over one long edge to the wrong side and iron in a crease. Fold and iron the two short sides in the same manner.

3. With right sides together, stitch the facing to the center of the sleeve edge (Fig. 4.15). Clip to the seam as shown. Fold the facing around to the wrong side of the sleeve, press along seam line, and blindstitch around folded edges of facing (Fig. 4.16).

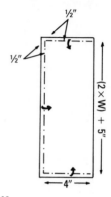

½"

½"

$(2 \times W) + 5"$

4"

4.14

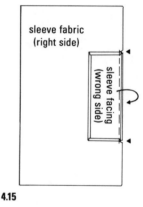

sleeve fabric (right side)

sleeve facing (wrong side)

4.15

sleeve fabric (wrong side)

sleeve facing (right side)

4.16

Sleeve Facings (Lined Garment)

Add sleeve facings (*sodegu-chi-gire*) to a fully lined garment when you wish to have the facing match the outer fabric of the garment. Otherwise, if a contrast is desired, the lining alone should be sufficient. In addition to a facing at the wristhole, a facing may also be attached to the body side of the sleeve opening on longer sleeves such as flutter sleeves (*furisode*).

1. Cut out two facings, one for each sleeve, to the dimensions shown in Figure 4.14.

2. Temporarily position the facing on the sleeve lining edge (Fig. 4.17). Reposition the facing parallel to its temporary position (Fig. 4.18). With right sides together, stitch the facing to the lining fabric.

3. Press the facing ends under ½" to the wrong side (Fig. 4.18). Fold the facing over along the seam line and press along the seam (Fig. 4.19).

4. Blindstitch the facing ends in place and baste the raw edge to the lining (Fig. 4.20). Continue with step 5, or go on to the rest of the garment from this point on, treating the sleeve lining and attached facing as one piece.

5. To add a facing to the body side of the sleeve (if it opens there, as in women's garments; Fig. 4.21), cut out four back sleeve facings, two for each sleeve, as shown in Figure 4.22. The facing should be long enough to reach from the bottom of the sleeve to 2" above the point where the sleeve will attach to the body.

6. Referring to Figures 4.17–20, follow the basic method outlined above to attach the facings.

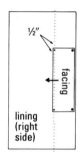

4.17

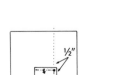

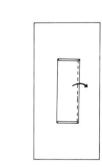

4.18

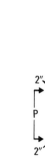

4.19

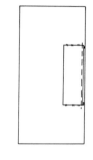

4.20

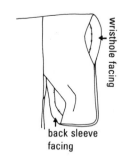

4.21

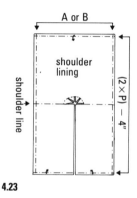

4.22

Shoulder Lining

The shoulder lining (*kata-suberi*) is sewn in when the garment is complete except for the addition of the collar. Use a lightweight, smooth fabric of a color that won't show through the face fabric.

1. Cut out one pattern piece as shown in Figure 4.23. The shoulder lining is as wide as the shoulder seam (A or B) and extends to about 2"–3" above the point where the sleeve attaches to the body (Fig. 4.26).

4.23

2. Turn under the front and back edges ½" and blindstitch or machine-baste (Fig. 4.24).

3. Turn under the side edges ½" and press (Fig. 4.25).

4. Sew the shoulder lining to the garment along the center back seam allowance (Fig. 4.27). Be sure to attach the bottom center point securely to the garment seam allowance. If there is no center back seam, allow the lining to hang freely.

5. Baste the side edges of the lining to the side seam allowances of the garment. Make sure all the points marked by dots are securely tacked (Figs. 4.26, 4.27). Baste the lining to the garment around the collar line.

Seat Lining

The seat lining (*ishiki-ate*) is simply a rectangle of smooth fabric positioned where friction occurs as the fabric moves up and down at the rear of the garment. Any scrap of smooth fabric will do. In fact, you often see thin cotton *tenugui* (hand towels) printed with a shop's name and phone number recycled in seat and shoulder linings.

1. Cut out one pattern piece to the following dimensions: The length should be equal to the distance from the small of the back to mid-thigh when the garment is on. The width is two-thirds the width of the garment (Fig. 4.28).

2. Turn under all raw edges ½", press, and blindstitch (Fig. 4.28).

3. Position seat lining on body, wrong sides together. With a holding stitch, sew the seat lining in place along the center back seam allowance (Fig. 4.29). Add a reinforcing line

of stitching within the center back seam allowance, ⅛"–¼" from the seam line. Be sure to securely tack the top and bottom of the lining in place (Fig. 4.30).

4. Open up the garment and lay it out flat. Spread the lining out flat and pin in place. Blindstitch the top and side edges to the garment, leaving the bottom edge unstitched (Fig. 4.30).

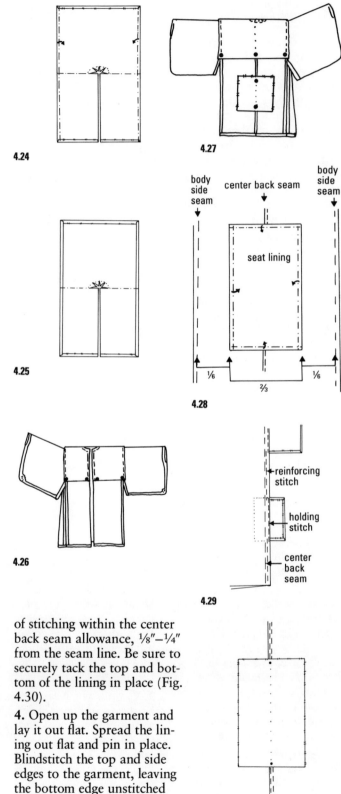

4.24

4.27

4.25

body side seam   center back seam   body side seam

seat lining

⅙   ⅔   ⅙

4.28

4.26

reinforcing stitch

holding stitch

center back seam

4.29

4.30

5 Sleeves

袖つけ

Sleeves are one of the more distinctive and important elements of Japanese clothing. They come in a great variety of widths and shapes; in fact, many garments derive their name from the type of sleeve they sport. The three basic types of sleeve are: squares, rectangles, and cones. Each type can be modified by rounding the bottom outside corner to varying degrees.

As a general rule, the sleeves on women's garments aren't attached along the entire body–sleeve seam and are open from the point where they leave the body (see Figs. 5.1–5) whereas men's sleeves are fully attached or closed from the point where they leave the body (see Figs. 5.6–11). The opening on women's sleeves helps prevent binding when the obi is worn. Women's sleeves also tend to come in sizes and shapes that "flutter" a bit more than men's do.

Other, more important criteria for selecting sleeve shape include comfort, convenience, and suitability to task. You would hardly plan to put flowing *furisode* sleeves (Fig. 5.3) on a work jacket, whereas if your goal is to catch someone's eye on a sunny spring day, nothing could be more effective. Similarly, while the gap under the sleeve of a woman's kimono allows tantalizing glimpses of a colorful lining or under-

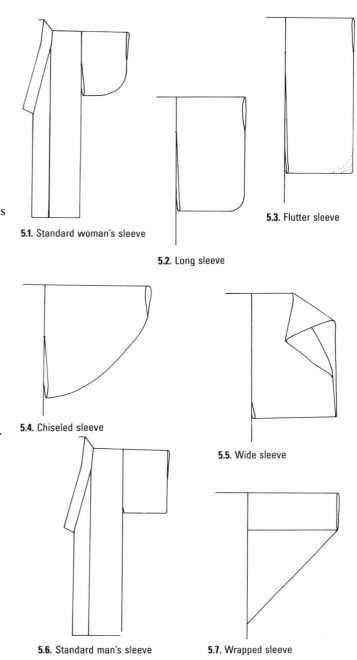

5.1. Standard woman's sleeve

5.2. Long sleeve

5.3. Flutter sleeve

5.4. Chiseled sleeve

5.5. Wide sleeve

5.6. Standard man's sleeve

5.7. Wrapped sleeve

kimono when worn Japanese-style, such a gap may be impractical for most styles of Western wear. There is no need to follow Japanese fashion conventions in the West—in fact, altering them with creative construction and wear can be much of the fun—although you should be aware that you might raise some Japanese eyebrows in the process.

Figures 5.1–11 illustrate the basic sleeve types. Dotted lines indicate possible variations in shape. "Flutter sleeves" (*furisode*; Fig. 5.3), are considered the most decorative and, accordingly, are worn on very formal occasions and sewn from beautiful Jacquard silk. Less exaggerated in length are "long sleeves" (*nagasode*; Fig. 5.2), and the standard "Genroku sleeves" (*genroku sode*; Fig. 5.1); both are long enough to be dressy, yet are more commonly worn when paying visits or taking a stroll on a bright sunny day. Men tend to wear squared sleeves, such as that in Figure 5.6, for all occasions. This is thought to be in keeping with a masculine look.

As the garment design shifts to work clothes, the sleeves become narrower and more rounded. Two examples are "chiseled sleeves" (*sogisode*; Fig. 5.4), and "boat-bottom sleeves" (*funazoko sode*; Fig. 5.9). Garments worn around the house or traditional workplace sport these sleeves. As the work becomes more active, the sleeves become even more tapered, such as evidenced in "wrapped sleeves" (*makisode*; Figs. 5.7, 5.8) and "tube sleeves" (*tsutsu-sode*; Figs. 5.10, 5.11). Women's *hippari* sleeves are often cinched at the wrist with elastic to keep them from getting caught on things.

The size of the wrist opening may be varied to suit specific needs. The "wide sleeve" (*hirosode*; Fig. 5.5) is open along the full width of the sleeve, allowing for freer arm movements. This sleeve is often found on the style of *hanten* jacket worn by women when carrying a baby piggyback (the jacket goes over mother and child). The wide wrist opening on the sleeves of summer *jimbei* tops encourages increased air circulation.

The most common width for sleeves in both men's and women's garments is one-third the body length (Figs. 5.1, 5.6). Women's sleeves are designed to end at the wrist (Fig. 2.13), while men's normally extend to a point about two-thirds the distance between the elbow and wrist (Fig. 2.14). In general, wider fuller sleeves are considered more formal and decorative, while narrower, tubelike or conical sleeves that taper in toward the wrist are more suitable for work or active lifestyles.

A subtle but important element of sleeve design is the question of how much of the sleeve is actually sewn to the body. On most work clothes, perhaps for reasons of practicality, the sleeves are attached to the body along their entire width. On more formal wear, i.e. kimono and *haori* jackets, the distance is determined by sex. Women's sleeves are usually attached along a distance equal to P, while men's are attached along 2 (or 1½) × P (Fig. 5.12).

Beyond this point, there is often some sleeve left hanging. When this occurs in a man's garment, the extending portion of sleeve is usually sewn closed. This extension rarely exceeds 2" in traditional men's

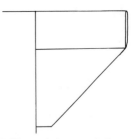

5.8. Wrapped sleeve variation

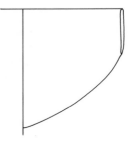

5.9. Boat-bottom sleeve

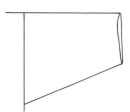

5.10. Tube sleeve

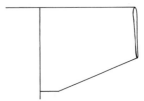

5.11. Tube sleeve variation

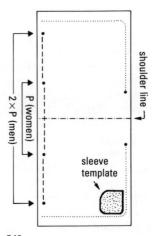

5.12

garments. In a woman's garment, however, the hanging portion of sleeve is finished off and allowed to remain open, exposing a glimpse of the lining or sleeve facing. The extension may be much longer than that of a man's sleeve, ranging up to as much as two feet or more in some flutter sleeves.

There are many styles of sleeve and many ways of constructing them. Below are basic instructions for the more common varieties.

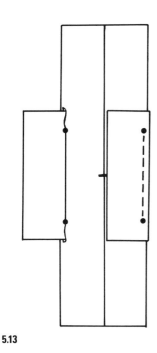

5.13

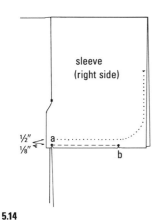

sleeve
(right side)

½″
⅛″
a
b

5.14

BASIC SLEEVE CONSTRUCTION

1. Transfer critical points on pattern to the wrong side of the fabric using straight pins, tailor's chalk, or a marking stylus. Use a sleeve template to delineate smooth corner curves (Fig. 5.12). The distance between the dots is P for women and 2 (or 1½) × P for men.

2. Stitch sleeve to garment body between dots (Fig. 5.13).

3. With wrong sides of sleeve together, sew along the sleeve bottom between points *a* and *b* (Fig. 5.14). Point *b* is where the sleeve curve begins. Clip to both points.

4. Turn sleeve inside out, so right sides are together (Fig. 5.15). Sew between points *c* and *d*; this completes the French seam begun in step 3. Next, sew between the following points in the order listed: *e* to *f* to *g*; and *h* to *i*. The stitching will overlap between points *d* and *h* and points *i* and *g*.

5. With tailor's chalk or a marking stylus, draw a straight line (*j* to *k*) as shown in Figure 5.16. Beginning at *j*, baste to *k*.

6. Then double back and baste a parallel line ⅛″ inside the first line (Fig. 5.17).

7. With the front side of the sleeve facing you, pull the thread from both ends to gather the material until the gathered corner lies relatively flat against the sleeve (Fig. 5.18). Position the gathers on the sleeve's front side, rolling the seam along the edge of the sleeve over to the front side. Knot the thread ends securely.

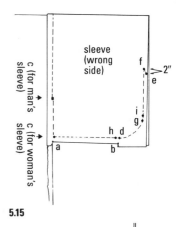

sleeve
(wrong side)

c (for man's sleeve)
c (for woman's sleeve)

f
e 2″
i
g
h d
a
b

5.15

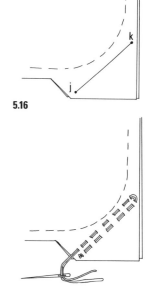

k
j

5.16

5.17

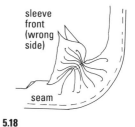

sleeve front
(wrong side)

seam

5.18

8. To position the seam properly, insert your thumb into the curve of the sleeve and ease the fabric into place. Do this with your left hand while pulling gently on the corner of the gathered seam allowance with your right hand (Fig. 5.19). Positioning the seam slightly ($1/16''$–$1/8''$) on the front of the sleeve will lend a softer, more pleasing line to the finished sleeve.

9. Position the sleeve template under the gathers. With a steam iron, gently flatten the gathers (Fig. 5.20). Avoid ironing the edge of the sleeve. For unlined garments, see Finishing Off the Unlined Sleeve (below).

To increase the size of the corner curve: Follow steps 1–9 above, except in steps 5 and 6 add another double line of basting halfway between the curve of the sleeve and the first line of basting (Fig. 5.21). The inner line somewhat follows the curve of the sleeve, the outer line is straight.

To further increase the corner curve: Follow steps 1–9 above, except in steps 5 and 6 add two more double lines of basting as shown in Figure 5.22. The innermost line follows the curve of the sleeve,

the next line is slightly less curved, and the outermost line is straight.

Other Sleeves

Follow the basic principles above, but construct the bottoms of the sleeves as shown in Figures 5.23–28. For wrapped-sleeve instructions, see *Hanten* Jacket (p. 76).

5.21

Finishing Off the Unlined Sleeve

For man's garment: Below the sleeve, press open and then tack down the body seam allowance with a blindstitch. Press open the seam allowance around the armhole and tack down with a blindstitch. Roll under the raw edge of the wrist opening and blindstitch in place. Figure 5.29 shows finished sleeve.

For woman's garment: With a blindstitch, hem unsewn edge of sleeve below dots. Press and tack seams and finish off wrist opening as for man's garment above. Figure 5.30 shows finished woman's sleeve. Add a reinforcement stitch at three points: where the side seam begins under the sleeve and where the sleeve joins the body on front and back (Fig. 5.31).

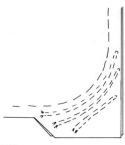

5.22

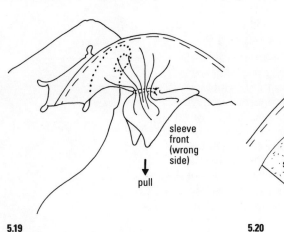

sleeve front (wrong side)

↓ pull

5.19

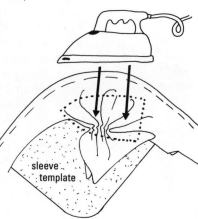

sleeve template

5.20

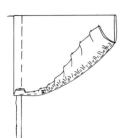

5.23, 5.24. Constructing a boat-bottom sleeve

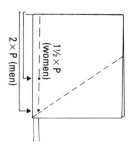
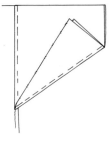

5.25, 5.26. Constructing a tube sleeve

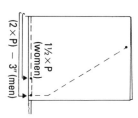
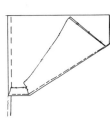

5.27, 5.28. Constructing a tube sleeve variation

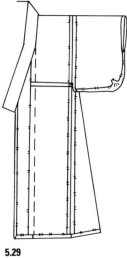

5.29

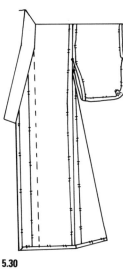

5.30

5.31

6 Hems

裾くけ

This chapter describes hems on unlined garments. Most lined garments, such as the kimono, *hanten* jacket, and *hippari* top, do not require hemming in the usual sense. The bottom edge of a lined garment is usually finished off by sewing the fabric to the lining, right sides together, straight across the bottom. The garment is then turned right-side out. The chapter "Linings" explains this method. Exceptions, notably the hems for lined outer robes and *haori* jackets, are covered under the specific garments.

ON UNLINED GARMENT

To sew the bottom hem of any unlined garment, start with the corners.

1. Fold and pin both bottom corners as shown in Figures 6.1–4.

2. Blindstitch one corner closed (Figs. 6.5–7).

3. Continue blindstitching the bottom hem to the opposite corner (Figs. 6.8–10) and blindstitch it closed (Figs. 6.11–13).

4. Knot the thread at the corner and take a stitch (Fig. 6.14) before trimming the thread end. Once the bottom edge is hemmed, blindstitch in a like manner from each corner up to the point where the collar will be attached.

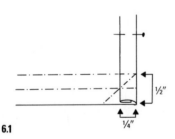

6.1

½"

¼"

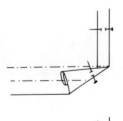

6.2

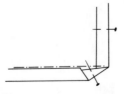

6.3

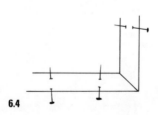

6.4

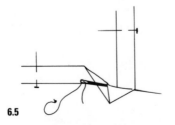

6.5

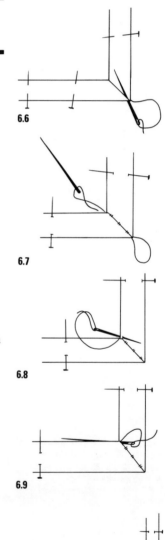

6.6

6.7

6.8

6.9

6.10

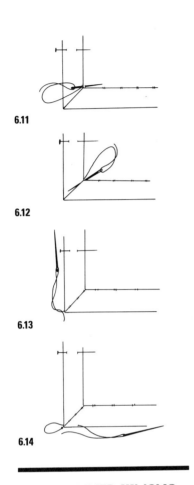

6.11

6.12

6.13

6.14

ON UNLINED KIMONO

On an unlined kimono, the overlap corners are usually finished off with a neat, origami-like fold as explained below.

1. Iron in the folds shown in Figure 6.15.

2. Open up the folds and insert the needle as shown in Figure 6.16.

3. Bring points *a* and *b* together and knot the thread (Figs. 6.17, 6.18).

4. Stitch from the knot at *a*/*b* to point *c* (Fig. 6.19); knot the thread end.

5. Fold the corner as shown in Figures 6.20 and 6.21.

6. Fold the garment edges along the creases (Fig. 6.22).

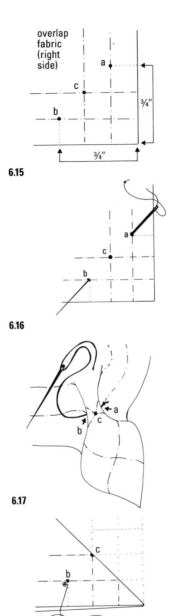

6.15

6.16

6.17

6.18

The corner should appear as in Figure 6.23.

7. Carefully turn the corner right-side out, iron, and baste down the hem edge approximately 5″ in both directions (Fig. 6.24). Hem the garment as usual from corner to corner, and then up to the bottom of the collar. Remove the basting when the hem is complete.

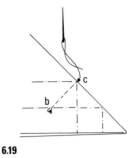

6.19

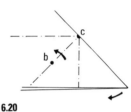

6.20

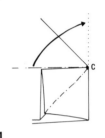

6.21

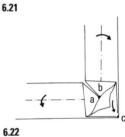

6.22

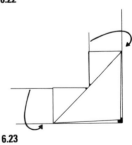

6.23

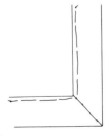

6.24

7 Collars

襟つけ

Four basic types of Japanese collar are presented here, classified by the way they lie against the body. The first type stands up behind the neck and curves around to lie flat at the front opening of the garment (Fig. 7.1). This collar is commonly found on garments that don't overlap at the front, such as vests and *han-ten* jackets.

The second type is also found on open-front garments, in particular the *haori* jacket, but it folds back on itself and lies flat on the body fabric of the garment, somewhat as a Western collar or lapel does (Fig. 7.2). Construction includes loops through which decorative cords are attached to close the jacket.

The third type of collar is used when the front panels of a garment overlap, as with the various kimono (Fig. 7.3). This collar stands up behind the neck and curves around to lie flat.

The fourth type resembles the kimono collar, except it is wider and lined (Fig. 7.4). This collar is found on outer robes and, less commonly, formal kimono.

Below are instructions for making these four basic collars and a replaceable collar cover (*kake-eri*) designed to protect the collar from wear and soiling. In addition, nontraditional collar shapes are introduced in some of the variation drawings at the end of each garment's instructions.

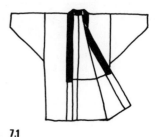

7.1

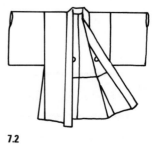

7.2

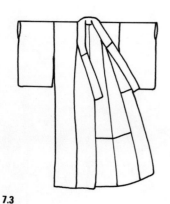

7.3

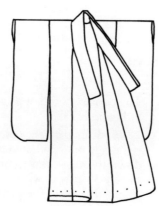

7.4

HANTEN JACKET OR VEST COLLAR

1. Determine your neck size (see p. 15) and transfer your neck shape to the fabric with tailor's chalk or a marking stylus (Fig. 7.5). Extend the side lines of the template straight down to the bottom of the body front (Fig. 7.6).

2. Determine the size of the collar piece as follows: Decide how wide you would like the finished collar to be (2″ to 2¼″ is typical) and multiply that figure by 4. The result is the width of the collar piece you will cut out. If you are small or prefer narrower collars, you may want a finished collar 1¾″ wide. In this case, you will need a strip of cloth 7″ wide (1¾″ × 4 = 7″). To determine the length of the collar strip, measure from the center back of the neck down to the bottom front; multiply by 2 and add an extra 3″–6″ to this measurement (Fig.

7.7). If necessary, the collar may be pieced together with smaller strips; try to plan such piecing so the seams will be hidden by the collar guard.

3. Iron the collar piece in half lengthwise, wrong sides together (Fig. 7.8). Open it up and with wrong sides together fold the long edges in to the center line, ironing them in place (Fig. 7.9).

4. Open the body front opening and spread the front pieces so the collar seam line forms a straight line (Figs. 7.10, 7.11). Unfold the collar piece and match its center point at fold line I with the center point of the back neck line, right sides of fabric together (Fig. 7.12). Pin the collar at fold line I to the body along the sewing line, beginning at the center point and working toward the bottom front on both sides. With a running stitch sew through all layers ¹⁄₁₆″–⅛″ inside the fold line, starting from the center point and stopping when you reach the bottom edges of the front.

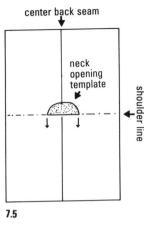

7.5

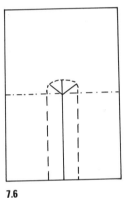

7.6

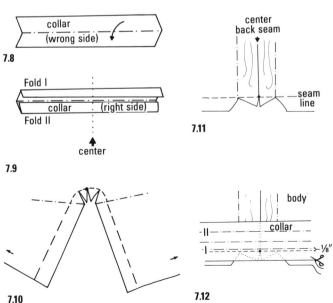

7.7

7.8

7.9

7.10

7.11

7.12

5. Refold the collar piece along the creases, sandwiching the body fabric in between. If the body fabric makes the collar too bulky, unfold the collar piece and trim off the excess body fabric (Fig. 7.12). Beginning at the center back, blindstitch the folded collar piece in place, sewing through collar fold and one layer of body fabric. The stitches should be invisible when viewed from either side of the collar. Temporarily stop sewing 3″ from the bottom hemmed front edge of the garment (Fig. 7.13).

6. Fold the extending collar ends up as shown in Figure 7.13, then fold collar back into place (Fig. 7.14). Resume stitching from step 5 and sew to bottom edge of garment. Continue, sewing bottom edge of collar closed with a slipstitch, and knot off thread when you reach the bottom front corner of the garment.

7. Attach collar guard (see below).

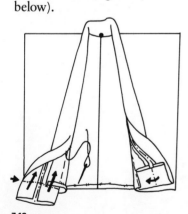

7.13

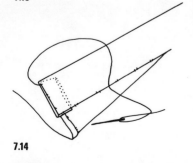

7.14

HAORI JACKET COLLAR

1. Follow steps 1–2 for *Hanten* Jacket or Vest Collar.

2. Iron the collar piece in half lengthwise, wrong sides together. Open it up and fold the long edges toward the center line as shown in Figure 7.15, ironing them in place.

3. Follow step 4 for *Hanten* Jacket or Vest Collar.

4. To make the loops: Cut two rectangles, each measuring 1″ × 3″, from the same fabric as used for the collar. To machine-sew, fold loop in half lengthwise and stitch together ¼″ from raw edges; turn inside out. To handsew, turn under the long sides ¼″ to the wrong side. Then slipstitch the folds together. See Figures 7.16–18.

5. Fold each loop as shown in Figure 7.19, overlapping ends. Tack together at the edges.

6. Pin the loops to the wrong side of the body front (Fig. 7.20) so the tacks are just inside the sewing line, loop end away from collar, and aligned with the bottom of P (the base of the ribcage; see Fig. 2.2) for men and the midpoint of P for women. See Figure 7.22.

7. Follow steps 5 and 6 for *Hanten* Jacket or Vest Collar, except stitch ¼″ to the inside of fold II. Note that the bottom edge of the garment (if it's a *haori* jacket) will not be parallel to the bottom edge of the collar (Figs. 7.21, 7.22) because the front body panel is cut at an angle.

8. The collar is worn properly by folding it back at the neck as you would a Western shirt

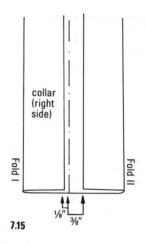

collar (right side)

Fold I · Fold II

⅛″ ⅜″

7.15

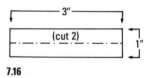

3″ (cut 2) 1″

7.16

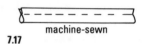

machine-sewn

7.17

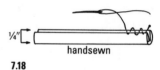

¼″ handsewn

7.18

½″

7.19

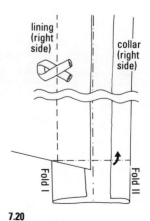

lining (right side) collar (right side)

Fold I · Fold II

7.20

collar. This causes the collar below the neck to fall open, somewhat like the lapel on a sports coat, all the way down to the front hem. Since the inner half of the collar is wider, the loops are partially concealed and the collar tends to remain open and flat. Figure 7.23 shows the folded collar from the inside of the garment.

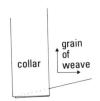

7.21

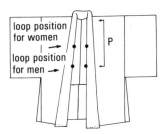

7.22

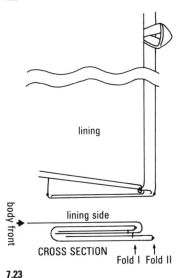

7.23

KIMONO COLLAR

The collar is the last part of a kimono to be sewn in place. Follow these instructions *after* stitching all major seams, setting in the sleeves, adding a lining (optional), and hemming the garment.

1. Determine the size of the collar piece as follows: Decide how wide you would like the finished collar to be (2½" is standard); multiply that figure by 3 and add ½". The result is the width of the collar piece to be cut out. (Hand measurement W is used in the patterns since it approximates the average collar width.) To determine the length of the collar piece, measure from the center back of the neck around the front down to the midpoint of the garment front; multiply by 2 and add an extra 6"–10". See Figure 7.24.

2. Align the center of the collar with the center back seam of the body, right sides together. Beginning at the center back, sew down to where the overlap is attached to the body, keeping the tension even between the body fabric and the collar, with a ½" collar seam allowance.

3. From this point on you will sew across the overlap angling toward the center point (Fig. 7.24) along the line shown in Figure 7.25. Ease about 3½" of the collar into the first 3" of the overlap. You may want to staystitch along this angled overlap sewing line before attaching the collar to keep the overlap from stretching out. Sew the rest of the collar to the overlap. Repeat this step for the other half of the collar.

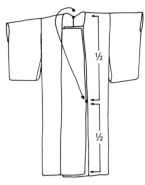

7.24

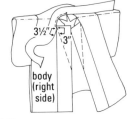

7.25

4. Fold the collar away from the body along the seam line. Iron in a crease on the collar $\frac{1}{16}$″ from the actual stitching (Fig. 7.26).

5. Fold under the unsewn edge of the collar at a line $\frac{1}{4}$″ less than one-third the width of the collar (Fig. 7.27). Press in the fold (Fig. 7.28).

6. Fold the collar in half lengthwise, sandwiching the body fabric in between. Pin, and then blindstitch in place, finishing off the bottom of the collar as in Figures 7.29–32.

7. Attach a collar guard (see below).

OUTER ROBE COLLAR

Outer robes (*uchikake*) always have this kind of collar—a lined collar designed for use on a lined garment. To wear this type of collar, fold it in half to the inside. Outer robes are usually made of stiff fabric, which keeps the collar in place once it's folded, but you may wish to lightly tack it down or sew in fabric-covered snaps to help it maintain its shape. The traditional method is to sew a silk thread to the body and collar edge as shown in Figure 7.33. To hold the collar closed, pull the threads in opposite directions.

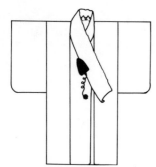

7.26

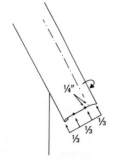

7.27

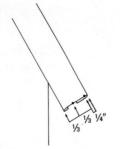

7.28

7.29

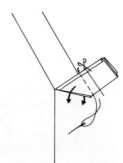

7.30

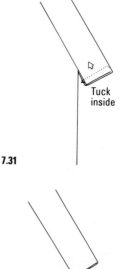

Tuck inside

7.31

7.32

The collar will appear as in Figure 7.34. Allow the threads to dangle inside the kimono while in use. To fold away the robe, loosen the threads gently until it looks like Figure 7.33 again.

1. Follow steps 2–4 for Kimono Collar, using collar patterns from Figures 9.3 (fabric) and 9.5 (lining).

2. With right sides together, sew a collar of lining fabric to the collar along the long unsewn edge (Fig. 7.35). The lining collar piece is 2″ narrower than the fabric collar piece and 44″ shorter. Stop sewing 10″ from what will be the bottom of the collar (Fig. 7.35). Iron a crease in the collar fabric 1″ from this seam

line; this will create a border of face fabric on the inside of the collar (Fig. 7.36).

3. Turning under the raw edge of the collar lining as you go, blindstitch the collar lining to the body lining, stopping about 10″ from what will be the bottom of the collar (Fig. 7.36).

4. Fold the excess face fabric at the collar ends to the lining side, angling in the corner as shown in Figures 7.37 and 7.38. Tuck the angled flap under the edge of the collar lining (Figs. 7.38, 7.39). Turn under the raw edge of the lining and press in the creases (Figs. 7.39, 7.40). Blindstitch all edges as shown in Figure 7.40.

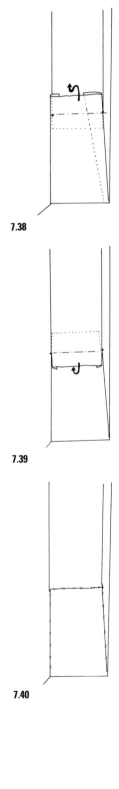

7.38

7.39

7.40

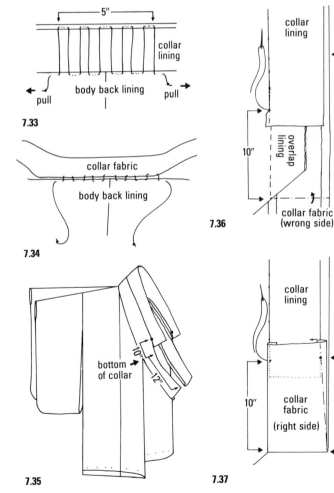

7.33

7.34

7.35

7.36

7.37

COLLAR GUARD

On informal jackets and vests as well as on kimono, an additional layer of cloth is commonly sewn over a portion of the collar to protect it from wear and soilage. This replaceable collar guard is called a *kake-eri*. You may use the same fabric used for the collar or something different. Japanese often use black plain-weave fabric or black velveteen for the collar guard of winter jackets. When the collar cover becomes soiled or torn, pull out the blindstitching to remove it. Then launder and restitch, or replace it with a new cover.

For Jacket or Vest

1. Determine the dimensions of the collar guard as follows: With pins mark the collar at a point two-thirds of the way down from the shoulder line to the hemmed edge (Fig. 7.41). Spread out the collar so it forms a straight line and measure between the pins. To this measurement add 1″; this is the length of the collar cover piece including seam allowance (Fig. 7.42). Multiply the collar width by 2 and add 1″; this is the width of the

cover piece including seam allowance. Cut out a rectangle of fabric to these dimensions. If using velveteen or some other fabric with nap, piece the collar guard from two strips of fabric; join the pieces at the ends with the nap going in opposite directions, so the nap will run down both sides of the front in the same direction.

2. Fold under and iron a ½″ hem around all edges, wrong sides together (Fig. 7.42). Fold entire piece in half lengthwise.

3. Matching centers of collar and collar guard, pin collar guard in place around collar, right side of fabric facing out. Blindstitch the guard to the collar (Fig. 7.43).

For Kimono

Follow the directions above, except adjust the length of the collar cover as follows: A woman's collar cover should reach to just barely above the top of her obi (Fig. 7.44). A man's collar cover should reach to a point about level with the bottom of his ribs (Fig. 7.45). For both men and women, the collar cover is nearly always made of the same fabric as the kimono itself.

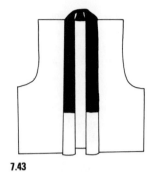

7.43

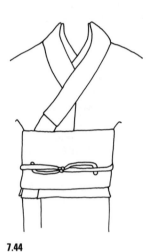

7.44

7.45

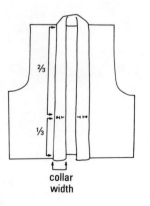

2/3

1/3

collar width

7.41

collar width × 2

center back

distance between pins on collar

7.42

PART THREE

The Garments

8 Kimono

着
物

In English, *kimono* is often used as a general term to refer to all Japanese or Asian clothing or any flowing gown. Indeed, in Japanese it literally means "things that are worn" or, simply put, "clothing." In this book, as in Japan, *kimono* refers to full-length Japanese clothing that overlaps in front (Figs. 8.1–4).

This includes *yukata*, typically of blue-and-white cotton prints, which are the garment of choice for attending summer festivals and firework displays, wandering through hot-spring towns, and strolling around a Japanese neighborhood on a hot summer's night. The *yukata* and its cousin the gauze-lined *nemaki* (a sleeping gown) are popular in the West as bathrobes or nightgowns.

More formal kimono are worn all year round, although the colors, patterns, and weight of the fabric vary with the season. These are the everyday dress of yesteryear that now are worn primarily on traditional, festive, or formal occasions such as tea ceremonies, weddings, funerals, and New Year's celebrations. These kimono were traditionally made of silk or wool, with or without a lining. Nowadays, like *yukata*, they are sewn from synthetic fabrics as well.

The same general pattern is used to make all types of

8.1, 8.2. Woman's kimono

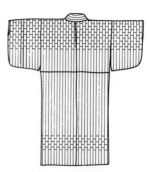

8.3, 8.4. Man's kimono

kimono. The pattern and construction do differ, however, depending on the sex of the wearer. Women's kimono are designed to be folded at the waist under a wide obi sash, so the garment drags on the floor if left open or if cinched without folding the fabric at the waist. The ideal proportions of a woman's kimono are shown in Figure 8.5; the kimono is as long as the woman is tall (head to toe) and as wide at the sleeves as her arms stretched out (fingertip to fingertip). When worn properly with an obi, a woman's kimono hangs to just slightly below the ankle. The side seams should line up right at the sides, the back seam should line up with the spine (you may choose to eliminate the center back seam if narrow Japanese fabric is not used), and the midpoint of the two front overlaps should line up with the center front of the body (Figs. 8.6, 8.7).

Donning traditional kimono and all the undergarments and accessories is so complex a process that nowadays it is taught in special classes and schools set up for this purpose; interested readers should consult such schools, a Japanese friend of the prewar generation, or *The Book of Kimono* for more details on wearing kimono in the traditional manner.

Men's kimono hang so that the hem just touches the floor when the garment is worn unbelted (Fig. 8.8). Addition of an obi shortens the kimono a bit, so the hem doesn't drag or get in the way. As with women's kimono, the back and side seams should align with the center back and center sides (Figs. 8.9, 8.10). Men's unlined kimono have a tuck sewn at the waist to

reduce stress on the fabric that results from not being folded at the waist. Unlike women's kimono, men's kimono have no opening under the arms. Women may find a man's kimono more practical for nontraditional wear (or more comfortable yet, lengthen the *hanten* jacket or *hippari* top).

Presented here are: a lined woman's kimono with long flutter sleeves (*furisode*); an unlined woman's kimono with Genroku sleeves; a man's lined kimono with Genroku sleeves; and the same man's kimono partially lined. When made of lightweight cotton, the unlined and partially lined kimono become *yukata*. *Yukata*, however, do not have flutter sleeves, as they are considered too dressy for this informal kimono. On a woman's *yukata*, substitute Genroku sleeves or some other shorter and narrower sleeve, such as boat-bottom sleeves or chiseled sleeves.

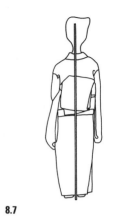

8.7

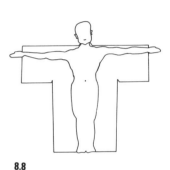

8.8

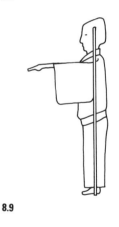

8.9

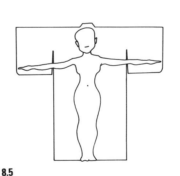

8.5

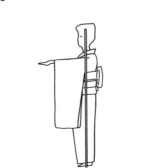

8.6

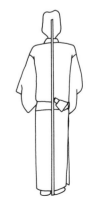

8.10

Materials

A lightweight cotton is the usual choice for summer kimono (*yukata*). Floral patterns are common for women's *yukata* and geometric patterns for men's *yukata*. For other seasons, a heavier cotton, wool, or silk is typical. A somewhat smooth flat weave, such as shantung, pongee, or *habutae* (often marketed under the name "habotae" in the U.S.), in a somber color, is appropriate for a man's kimono for formal occasions. Women's kimono tend toward a broader range of silk weaves including crepes and Jacquards that drape in softer, gentler lines and nubby weaves such as spun silk (*tsumugi*). Traditionally, lightweight cotton or silk was used for the lining. On a lined woman's kimono, you might wish to use a bright-colored contrasting fabric for the front and back hems and overlap hems. If you intend to make a matching formal *haori* jacket to wear over the kimono, remember to buy enough yardage for both kimono and jacket.

Ideas

To make a kimono blouse or dress, shorten the kimono body and overlaps to the desired length. Experiment with different sleeve shapes (see Sleeves, p. 29). To make the flutter sleeves less of a hazard, you might try these innovative designs: Keep the length but make them narrower, or gather them along the shoulder line and add shoulder padding. To keep the kimono hem out of the way, you might borrow a trick from Japanese travelers and itinerant performers—lift the bottom edge of the back hem and tuck it down between the obi and kimono (Figs. 8.11–13).

When vigorous activities are undertaken while wearing kimono, the sleeves are often tied out of the way with a cord called a *tasuki* (see box). Consider using a very decorative cord in this manner as part of your ensemble.

HOW TO TIE A TASUKI CORD

1

2

3

4

8.11

8.12

8.13

INSTRUCTIONS

Woman's Lined Kimono

1. Cut out the pattern pieces (Figs. 8.14–16), using measurements derived from Making the Pattern (p. 10). The sleeve pattern is for knee-length flutter sleeves. For shorter sleeves that extend to mid-hip, replace S with measurement R. Or, select a different sleeve shape and alter the pattern piece accordingly. Back sleeve and wrist facings are optional (see Sleeve Facings, p. 27).

2. Sew the fabric pieces labeled "hem" to the bottoms of the corresponding lining pieces (Fig. 8.17). From this point on, this fabric/lining will be referred to as "lining."

3. Sew a center back seam in lining and fabric by folding the body back in half lengthwise with right sides together, making sure the side edges match up evenly. Sew ½" from fold, stitching from top to bottom. Iron flat to either side.

4. Sew the right overlap to the right front, with right sides of fabric together; align the bottom edges and sew to the top (Fig. 8.18). Repeat for the left overlap. Press seam allowances of body front pieces to back, wrong sides together, along stitching line.

5. Make the sleeves and attach to the body, following steps 1–5 of Full Lining (p. 25).

6. Sew the body front to body back along the side seams, right sides together, between dots as indicated in Figure 8.19. Press seam open.

7. Follow steps 4 and 6 above for the lining body.

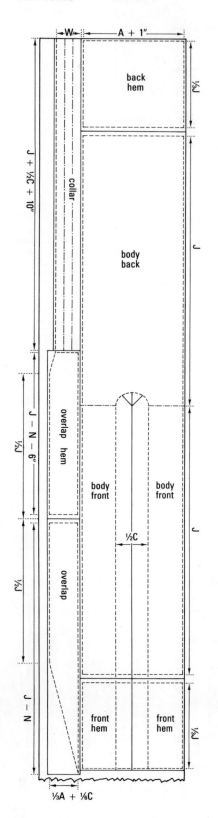

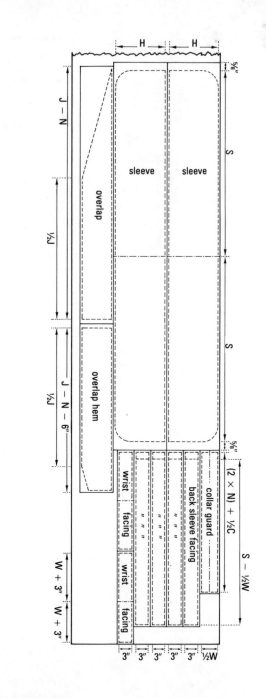

8.14, 8.15. Fabric

WOMAN'S KIMONO PATTERN

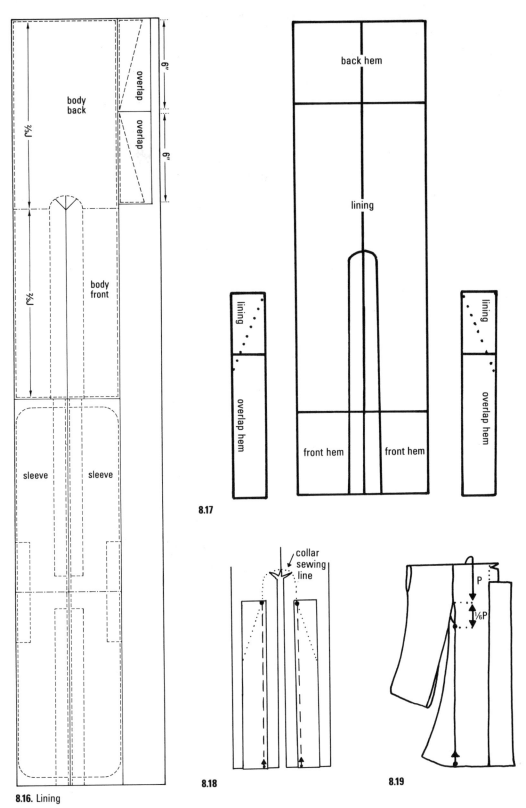

8.16. Lining

*Lining same as fabric except
where otherwise indicated.*

8.17

8.18

8.19

8. Sew the lining to the fabric at the hem: Align the hems, right sides together, taking care to match up the overlap, side, and center back seams. Continue to line the kimono, following steps 8–10 under Full Lining.

9. Sew on the collar, following directions under Kimono Collar (p. 39). The bottom of the collar should hit the exact middle of the garment (Fig. 8.20). Note, too, that if you've followed directions properly, the overlap and front body panel widths will be in a ratio of 2 to 3 (Fig. 8.20). Sew on the collar guard (see Collar Guard, p. 42).

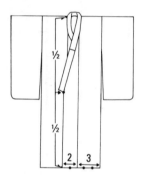

8.20

KIMONO VARIATIONS

1. "Roman" kimono. An unlined kimono with double casings sewn in at all seams except the collar and sleeve bottoms. Cords within the casings are pulled to gather the fabric, for a Roman curtain effect. The cords may be tied into bows, leaving the gathers adjustable, or stitched in position and trimmed.

2. Kimono blouse with boat-bottom sleeves. Shorten the regular woman's kimono (use measurement R instead of J for length) and add a box pleat at the small of the back to taper the waist. The blouse is shown tied with a *kaku* obi in a shell knot.

3. Ball gown. Cut all pieces of the regular woman's kimono in wedge shapes instead of rectangles. Notice how the back is cut longer than the front to form a train. A padded outer robe hem has been added for heightened drama. The sash is passed to the inside of the garment through the slit below the sleeves.

Variation **1**

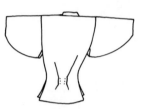

Variation **2**

Variation **2** (modeled)

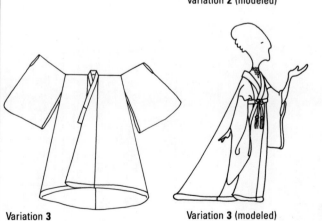

Variation **3**

Variation **3** (modeled)

Woman's Unlined Kimono

1. Cut out the pattern pieces, taking the body, overlap, collar, and collar guard from Figures 8.14 and 8.15 and the (Genroku) sleeves from Figure 8.22. Substitute H for I in the sleeves. Facings (Fig. 8.15) are optional (see Sleeve Facings, p. 26). Refer to Making the Pattern (p. 10).

2. Follow steps 3 and 4 for Woman's Lined Kimono.

3. Make the sleeves and attach to the body following steps 1–9 of Sleeves (p. 31).

4. Follow step 6 for Woman's Lined Kimono.

5. Press all seams flat. If raw edges (besides the hem and collar line) are exposed, turn or roll them under ⅛" and blindstitch flat to the garment body.

6. Hem the garment and roll the front overlap edge as outlined under Hems (p. 35).

7. Attach collar, following instructions for Kimono Collar (p. 39), and collar guard (see Collar Guard, p. 42).

Man's Lined Kimono

Fully pad this kimono with batting (see Padding, p. 20), and you have the perfect robe for snuggling up in front of the fireplace with a book on a cold winter evening.

1. Cut out the pattern pieces (Figs. 8.21–24), using measurements derived from Making the Pattern (p. 10). To add a full lining, replace the K + 5" measurement with K; lined garments do not have a tuck at the waist. The sleeves in the pattern layout will hit about belly-button level when the arms are stretched out. You may select a different shape, but remember to adjust the pattern pieces accordingly. If you are padding the kimono, boat-bottom or chiseled sleeves may be more comfortable than the Genroku sleeves presented.

2. Follow steps 3–9 for Woman's Lined Kimono.

Man's Unlined Kimono

1. Cut out the pattern pieces (Figs. 8.21, 8.22), using measurements derived from Making the Pattern (p. 10).

2. Follow step 3 of Woman's Lined Kimono.

3. Sew a seat lining (see Seat Lining, p. 28) to the wrong side of the body back, positioning it so that the top aligns with fold *a* (Fig. 8.25).

4. Fold body at lines *a* and *b* as shown (Fig. 8.26). Sew along line *a* and then line *b* with a backstitch. Fold along lines *c* and *d* in a similar manner and backstitch in place along lines *c* and *d*.

5. Follow step 4 of Woman's Lined Kimono. Note that there is no tuck in the overlap piece.

6. Follow step 3 of Woman's Unlined Kimono.

7. Follow step 6 of Woman's Lined Kimono. Side seams are not always pressed open. Often, especially in unlined men's garments, the following method is used to finish off the side seams: Instead of ironing the seam open, iron the seam allowance toward the garment front (toward the overlap) from the bottom to the point where the front and back tucks meet (Fig. 8.27). Rip out tuck stitching on body back from fabric edge to side seam. Fold the underarm

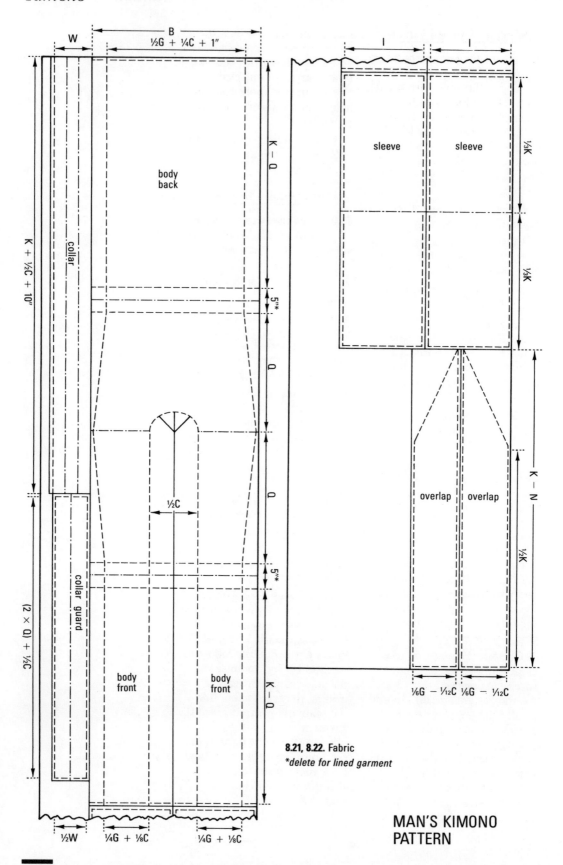

8.21, 8.22. Fabric
*delete for lined garment

**MAN'S KIMONO
PATTERN**

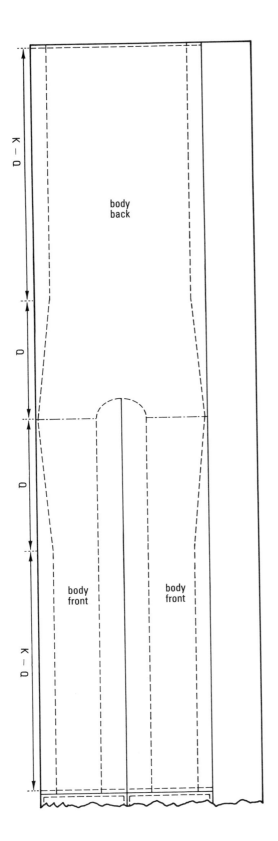

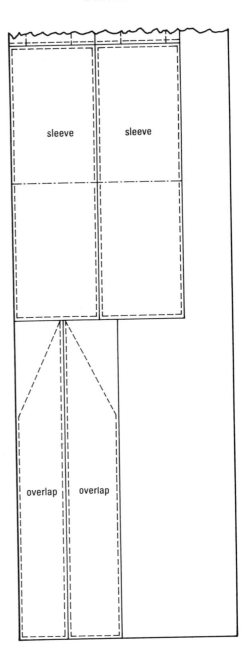

8.23, 8.24. Lining

Lining same as fabric except where otherwise indicated.

Kimono

area in an origami-like fashion, as shown in Figure 8.28, and press.

8. Follow steps 5 and 6 of Woman's Unlined Kimono.

9. Sew the shoulder lining in place following directions for Shoulder Lining (p. 27).

10. Follow step 9 under Woman's Lined Kimono. Figure 8.29 shows the finished inside of the kimono.

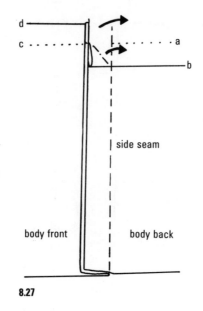

8.27

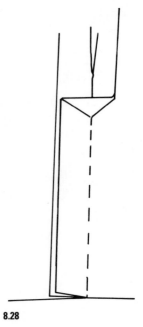

8.28

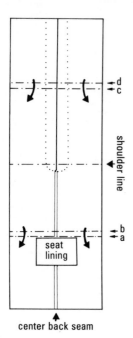

8.25

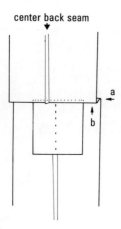

8.26

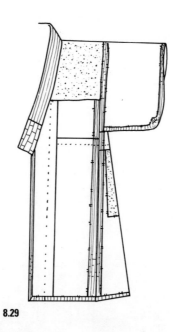

8.29

9 Outer Robe

Japanese women first began to wear this type of loose kimono over their *kosode* ("small-sleeved" kimono) and obi during the Kamakura period (1185–1336). Over the following two centuries, these loose kimono became very popular. In the Edo period (1603–1868) *uchikake*, as they were called, were *de rigueur* at formal occasions, and wives of feudal sovereigns wore them as part of their daily attire. Perhaps because they composed the outer layer, the one with the greatest expanse of fabric exposed to view, outer robes came to be woven and dyed in lavish colors and patterns. Indeed, outer robes are still considered the epitome of classical beauty.

Today the outer robe is worn by women almost exclusively as a beautiful wedding robe. A traditional wedding robe is sewn from pure white, figured silk satin. Just as white silk is a clean slate ready to be dyed, so, according to tradition, does the bride enter the groom's household ready to take on their "patterns and colors"—that is, the ways of his household.

In keeping with modern tastes, however, large bold colorful designs often decorate outer robes (Figs. 9.1, 9.2), with the focus of attention usually being drawn to the center back of the garment.

9.1, 9.2. Outer robe

Elaborate dyework and intricate embroidery depict felicitous symbols such as phoenixes, balls of fire, crane-and-turtle combinations, pine, bamboo, and plum motifs, and flower carts.

In construction, the outer robe is very similar to the kimono, with three notable exceptions: The collar is always backed with lining fabric, the hem line is heavily padded, and the collar extends only about two-fifths of the way down the garment. Another distinctive feature is that the lining extends several inches around the bottom hem to show on the front. The outer robe is always lined and never belted in Japan.

Materials

As befits the most elite of Japanese garments, traditional, narrow-width fabric is often dyed or woven specially for outer robes: The nonrepeating design is planned to match at the seams to form one overall dramatic picture. The fabric is always top-quality silk. The lining is commonly *chirimen* (a lightweight silk crepe), which, because it has more give than most fabrics, creates a lovely unpuckered roll at the hem.

Suitable substitutes that capture the elegance of the original include delicately detailed upholstery fabric and shiny fabrics (such as satin brocade) with large woven patterns. If you are lucky enough to find two matching obi (the *maru* obi type) at a flea market, you have the ideal fabric; the outer robe pictured on p. 60 was made from such a pair. For lining material, china silk works well as does

crepe de chine. Batting, wool or synthetic, is necessary for the padded hem.

Ideas

For nontraditional wear, you might wish to shorten the outer robe to ankle length, so it doesn't drag on the floor. The padding may be incorporated in the hems of other garments such as Kimono Variation 3 (p. 50). For a baby wrap, make a miniature, entirely padded version of the robe but substitute more practical sleeves, such as chiseled or tube sleeves, for the flutter sleeves in this pattern.

Traditionally, elaborate embroidery and couching have been popular surface decorations on outer robes. You can also achieve fine results using Western techniques such as surface quilting, trapunto, and appliqué. Smocking and crewelwork, or even hand painting and airbrushing, may be used to dramatic effect.

INSTRUCTIONS

1. Follow steps 1 and 3–7 of Woman's Lined Kimono (p. 47), except use the patterns shown in Figures 9.3–6.

2. Prepare the hem batting as follows: Cut a piece of batting about 12″–15″ wide and a little longer than the length of the hem (Fig. 9.7). Cut another piece the same length and about 8″–10″ wide. Feather all edges.

Twist a 5″ wide strip of batting (long enough to go around the hem), evening out the thickness as you go. When

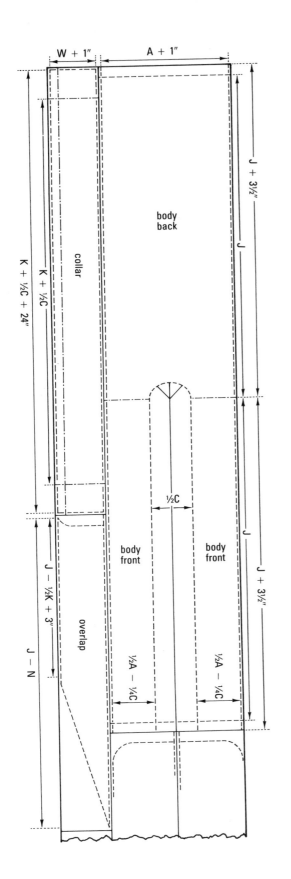

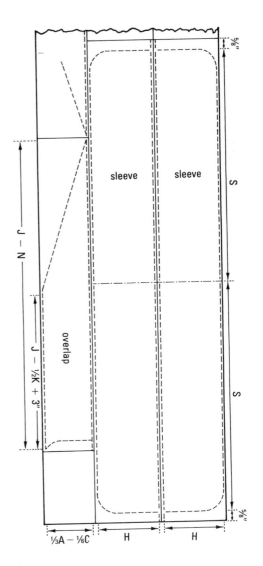

9.3, 9.4. Fabric

OUTER ROBE
PATTERN

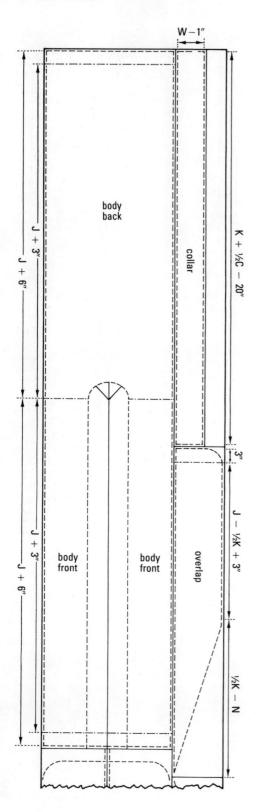

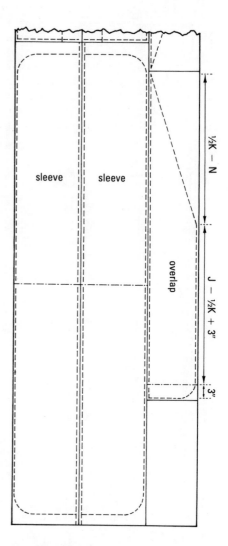

9.5, 9.6. Lining

Lining same as fabric except where otherwise indicated.

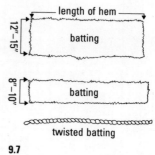

9.7

Traditional Japanese garments, while governed by strict rules of wear in Japan, are designed with enough fullness to allow great creativity in draping the human figure. This silk kimono is wrapped high off the floor with a diagonal front line for visual interest and ease in walking. Positioning the obi bow stylishly in front makes for more comfort when sitting in chairs. *(Instructions on p. 47.)*

The *yukata*, or unlined cotton kimono, has already attained a good measure of popularity in the West. You can sleep in one, throw it on after a bath or after work, or wear it to lend a festive touch to outdoor summer activities. While women traditionally wear an obi tied in back as shown here, a narrower sash is easier to tie and untie. *(Instructions on p. 51.)*

The kimono and its variations may well be the ultimate in lounge wear—it is hard to imagine any other garment that is simultaneously as comfortable and elegant. Here, an outer robe constructed from two matching silk brocade obi adds luxurious warmth and drama to a kimono worn in the loose style of the Heian nobility. *(Instructions on p. 56.)*

While designed as a coat to wear over kimono, the *haori* jacket makes an elegant evening wrap that fits easily over almost any Western garment. So gorgeous is the lining fabric that peeks through the sleeve openings that many women in the West wear these jackets inside out. *(Instructions on p. 73.)*

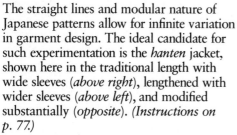

The straight lines and modular nature of Japanese patterns allow for infinite variation in garment design. The ideal candidate for such experimentation is the *hanten* jacket, shown here in the traditional length with wide sleeves (*above right*), lengthened with wider sleeves (*above left*), and modified substantially (*opposite*). (*Instructions on p. 77.*)

The blue jacket's design, commemorating the 25th anniversary of the Florin Japanese Language School in California, incorporates the school's logo (pine trees), crest, and colors in much the same way that traditional *hanten* bear the crest or other symbols of a merchants', firemen's, or artisans' association.

The red silk smoking jacket is based on the pattern for *Hanten* Jacket Variation 4 (p. 81). Protective guards at the pockets and cuffs absorb wear and serve as a design accent.

The wraparound *hippari* top is an excellent example of the versatility and practical comfort afforded by Japanese workclothes. Wear it as a blouse, jacket, or work smock. The front panels overlap and are held in place with two sets of ties. *(Instructions on p. 86.)*

The traditional padded vest, like a down vest, provides freedom of movement along with warmth. Although associated with children in Japan, it is suitable for all ages. The child's vest shown here is cut somewhat large to allow for growth. *(Instructions on p. 91.)*

Of the same basic construction as the *hippari* top, the *jimbei* is Japan's answer to hot weather. Open side seams joined only with decorative stitching, in combination with the loose wraparound fit, make this traditional man's top the perfect summer garment for both sexes. Here it is worn as a beach coverup. *(Instructions on p. 84.)*

Still worn by farm women and other workers in Japan, these roomy slacks have been rediscovered by modern Japanese fashion designers as comfortable, stylish wear for active people. Choose between a tie closing or an elasticized waist. *(Instructions on p. 98.)*

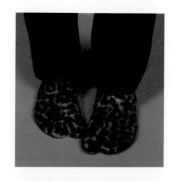

Creative fabric selection can lend a delightful range of personalities to the simple forms of Japanese clothing. Standard white tabi—two-toed socks worn with thonged footwear—dazzle the eye when made of brocade, become whimsical slippers when sewn of leopard-spotted fabric, and turn into stylish shoes when constructed of wool-lined leather. The rubber-soled, high-top indigo *jika-tabi* are a favorite among Japanese carpenters and tree trimmers, who find the sensitized grip unbeatable for maneuvering on ladders and scaffolding. *(Instructions on p. 109.)*

Any reputation the kimono has for being uncomfortable is more properly blamed on the wide constricting obi worn by women in recent centuries. This man's sash, a *kaku* obi, is recommended for both sexes as its moderate width is comfortable. The classic shell knot is easy to tie, lies flat against the body, and may be readily modified to achieve different looks, as demonstrated here with an Andean strap. *(Instructions on p. 104.)*

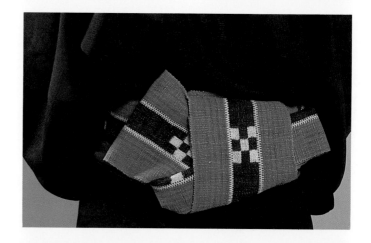

finished, grasp the ends and give it a gentle pull to compact the batting somewhat. Lay this cording slightly off-center on the narrower strip of batting, and fold over the batting, staggering the long edges a bit (Fig. 9.8).

3. Lay this piece so the twisted cording lies slightly off-center on the wider strip of batting (Fig. 9.9) and again fold in half, staggering the edges (Fig. 9.10). Staggering the edges helps reduce bulk along the top edge, rendering a more graceful taper. Set the batting aside for now.

4. Lay out the face fabric hem line, right-side up, to form a straight line. Lay the lining hem line on top, right-side down, matching up corresponding seams (Fig. 9.11). Position the lining 3″ above

the bottom edge of the fabric. Locate the center of each overlap piece and insert a straight pin at each center point. Sew the lining to the fabric between the pins.

5. Mark a point 3″ above the seam stitched in step 4 at both sides of the lining (Fig. 9.12). Bring each point down to the corresponding bottom corner of the face fabric. Ease the lining to form a gentle curved line, and stitch along this line between pin and corner dot (Fig. 9.13).

6. Turn the garment over. Pin together the top center back of the lining and fabric bodies. Pass a pole (or broomstick) through the sleeves to allow the layers to hang out properly (Fig. 9.14). The lining will extend lower than the fabric.

9.8

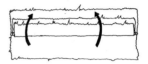

9.9

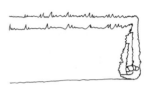

9.10

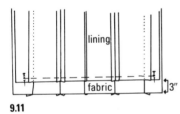

9.11

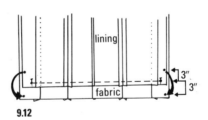

9.12

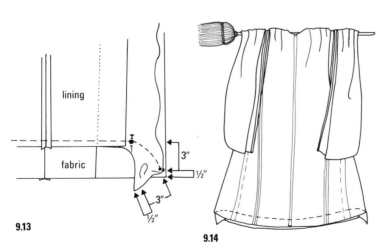

9.13

9.14

7. Fold the face fabric up along the stitching line, bringing the lining seam allowance with it, and press in place (Fig. 9.15). Make a tiny clip at the curves if the face fabric puckers as it is folded.

8. Follow steps 8 and 9 for Full Lining (p. 25). Then turn the entire garment right-side out.

9. Lay the prepared batting along the lower edge of the hem, folded edge down (Fig. 9.16). Trim the ends even with the length of the hem line and loosely sew the batting ends closed.

10. Carefully insert the batting between the lining and fabric at the collar opening and position it at the hem line along the rounded bottom of the lining. Using a holding stitch, sew through the fabric, batting, and lining to hold the batting in place (Fig. 9.17).

11. Sew on the collar, following the directions under Outer Robe Collar (p. 40). Note that

the robe collar does not extend as far down the front as a regular kimono collar does. A kimono collar extends about halfway down the garment front, while the outer robe collar extends only about two-fifths of the way down (Fig. 9.18). Accordingly, the bottom of the outer robe collar should line up with the bottom of the collar of a properly sashed woman's kimono (Fig. 9.19).

12. Since the outer robe is worn over several layers of garments, a collar guard is often omitted; the collar rarely comes into contact with the skin in the neck area, reducing the incidence of soilage. If you intend to wear the outer robe in a nontraditional manner, you might wish to incorporate a collar guard into the design, in which case the collar guard is stitched only to the face fabric of the collar and not wrapped to the lining side.

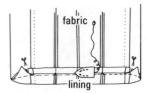

9.15

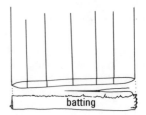

9.16

9.17

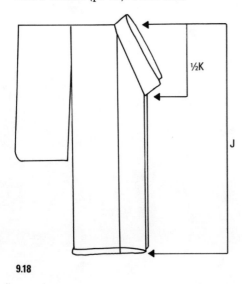

9.18

9.19

10 Haori Jacket

羽
織

The formal jacket (*haori*) is designed to be worn over a kimono for additional warmth. Some may even be lightly padded. Unlike the informal *hanten* jacket, the *haori* is not worn over casual clothes. A typical formal jacket is of black silk, with a family crest embroidered or dyed at one, three, or five points: the top center back; that plus one on each front panel; or all of the preceding plus one on the back of each sleeve. The more family crests, the more formal the garment.

A woman's jacket is also designed to match or complement the colors and patterns of the kimono over which it is worn (Fig. 10.1). A man's, on the other hand, is traditionally made of the same fabric as the kimono, although in summer a jacket of black gauze can be worn over any kimono (Fig. 10.2). Except for the see-through gauze style, *haori* for both sexes are usually lined. Indeed, one of the delights of formal jackets is the lining, which typically is a bright or beautifully woven, dyed, or decorated silk. The wearer is the only one aware of the lining's beauty, except when others catch a chance glimpse through the sleeve opening or when the *haori* is being put on or taken off.

Another arena for subtlely exerting your design personality is in the choice of ties to

10.1. Woman's *haori* jacket

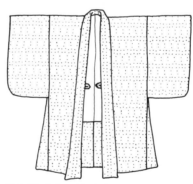

10.2. Man's *haori* jacket

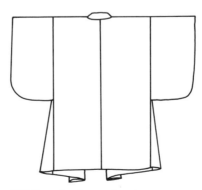

10.3. Rear view (woman's and man's *haori*)

attach to the front closing. Jacket ties (*haori himo*) come in a great variety of colors and shapes—tubular braids, flat weaves, double strands, etc.

In Japan a *haori* jacket is always worn over a kimono (except for kimono with flutter sleeves, in which case a shawl is worn) when one leaves the house. Etiquette dictates removing the jacket before entering a house. Before World War II, Japanese also removed their *haori* while in the presence of a very important person: People who went to see the emperor off on a trip always removed their *haori*—those in Western garb removed their coats—and kept them off until the train was out of sight, no matter how inclement the weather. (The trick was to wear long underwear under the kimono.)

Presented here are lined and unlined *haori* jackets, for women and men. Note that the collar is worn folded back; it lies flat somewhat like a Western collar. The jacket has side gussets, and the front body hem lines angle down from the side seams toward the center front opening.

The woman's jacket has the characteristic opening where the lower sleeve hits the body. The woman's Genroku sleeves reach to the base of the buttocks when her arms are stretched out horizontal. The man's jacket has slightly shorter Genroku sleeves, the most commonly seen shape on men's *haori*, and the body side seams taper in from the shoulders to the waist. The key point is having the *haori* sleeves large enough to fit over the kimono sleeves without causing them to bunch. Women who plan to wear the jacket over slacks or a dress should follow the sewing lines

MAN'S HAORI PATTERN

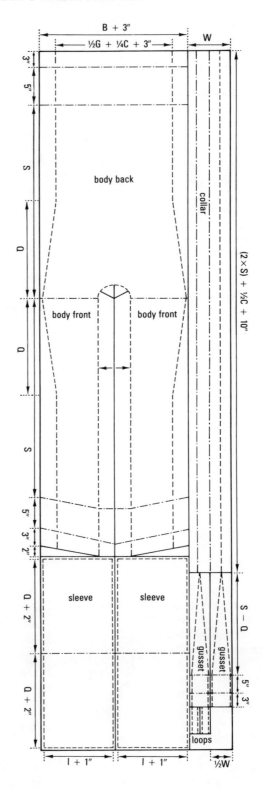

10.4. Fabric

for the man's jacket for a better fit. The woman's jacket is voluminous and best worn by larger body types or over a kimono and woman's obi.

Materials

Common choices are: for summer, silk organza or a sturdy gauze, unlined and usually black or navy blue; for spring and autumn, cottons or linens, lined or unlined; and for winter, woolens, lined. For a take-off on the gauze style of jacket, you might try using a lace tablecloth or silky rayon drapery fabric. For a man's jacket, if you are sewing a kimono as well, use the same fabric for the *haori* jacket. For lining, silk or synthetics are suitable. If you elect to pad the garment, you must also line it. You need two *haori* ties, which may be purchased in Japan at department stores and flea markets, in Japantowns abroad, and wherever second-hand *haori* are sold.

Ideas

The *haori* is frequently worn in the West as an elegant party jacket over a dress or blouse and slacks. Many people turn the *haori* inside out to show off the colorful lining. An unorthodox but attractive blouse can be fashioned from the *haori* as shown in Variation 4.

For ties, let your imagination be your guide: Braids and cords, colorful shoelaces, laniards, and crocheted ribbon are but a few of the possibilities. Or you may decide to omit the ties and fabric loops altogether and close the front with, say, a frog or five-yen piece (it has a hole in the middle) with a loop of cord.

INSTRUCTIONS

Man's Haori (Unlined)

1. Cut out the pattern pieces (Fig. 10.4), using measurements derived from Making the Pattern (p. 10). Sew in the center back seam, taking a ½" seam allowance.

2. With right sides together, sew the sleeve pieces to the body between the dots (Figs. 10.5). The dots are 4"–6" from the bottom of the sleeve fabric. Continue sewing the sleeves as directed under steps 3–9 of Sleeves (p. 31). The sleeves should angle in a bit toward the waist as they follow the body side seam line.

3. Sew the side gussets in place. Notice how the gusset sewing lines form a triangle. The peak of the triangle (*a*) should hit just under the point where the sleeve attaches to the body. Points *b* and *c*, at the bottom of the triangle formed, should fall on the hem line, fold line II (Figs. 10.6, 10.7). Sew from *a* to *b* and then to the bottom raw edge of the garment (Fig. 10.6). Sew from *a* to *c* and below, in a like manner. Press the gusset flat and blindstitch the seam allowance edges to the body (Fig. 10.7).

4. Fold the bottom raw edge up 3" to the wrong side along fold line I and up another 5" along fold II. Press in soft creases on the fold lines and blindstitch the hem in place (Fig. 10.8).

5. Sew in a shoulder lining as outlined under Shoulder Lining (p. 27).

6. Sew and attach the loops and collar as directed under *Haori* Jacket Collar (p. 38).

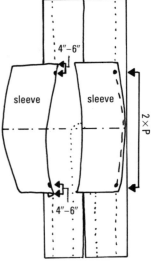

10.5

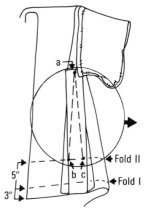

10.6

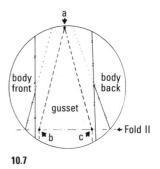

10.7

10.8

HAORI TIES

Most ties used to hold *haori* closed are *kumihimo*, or braided cord. You can make your own version of *kumihimo* with very small scale crocheting or spool knitting. Silk thread is best as it holds a knot well.

Women and men wear the same shape of ties—flat and tubular—but women's ties are smaller than men's. Women's ties are about ⅛"–¼" wide and 5"–7" long. Men's ties range from flat braids ½" wide and 12" long to thick round cords ⅜" in diameter and 15"–16" long. These measurements do not include tassels, pompoms, or loops at the ends of the braids.

All ties have a small loop at one end for attaching the tie to the *haori* jacket collar as shown in Figures 1 and 2. Alternatively, a small S hook (available at hardware stores) may be used to connect the tie loop to the jacket collar loop (Fig. 12). Once the cords are knotted together, you can open and close the garment at the hooks rather than undo an elaborately tied knot.

Directions for knotting a woman's and a man's set of ties are shown, respectively, in Figures 3–6 and Figures 7–12. (Figures 7–11 show the knot from the back; Figure 12 shows a front view of the finished knot.) These are just two examples of a wide variety of knots.

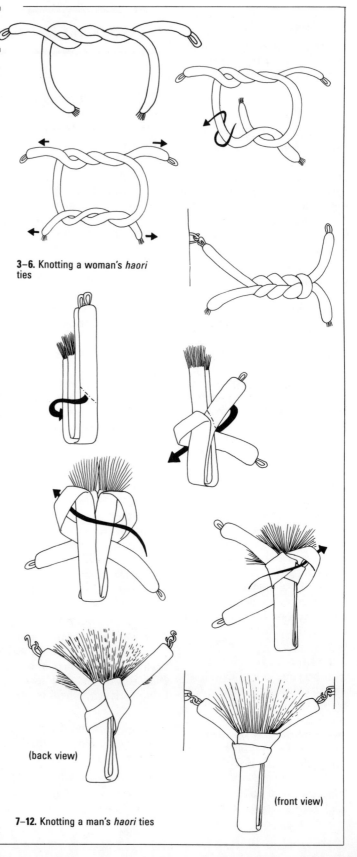

3–6. Knotting a woman's *haori* ties

(back view)

(front view)

7–12. Knotting a man's *haori* ties

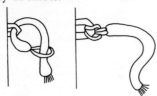

1, 2. Attaching a *haori* tie to the collar

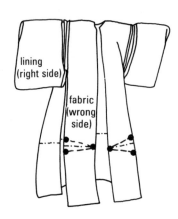

Woman's Haori (Lined)

1. Cut out the pattern pieces (Figs. 10.9, 10.10), using measurements derived from Making the Pattern (p. 10). If you intend to wear the jacket over a kimono, be sure to style the *haori* sleeves so that the kimono sleeves will fit inside without bunching. Sew in the center back seam (in lining and fabric), taking a ½″ seam allowance.

2. Follow steps 2–5 for Full Lining (p. 25). The garment should appear as in Figure 10.11.

10.11

3. Fold along the tuck fold lines (Fig. 10.11) as shown in Figure 10.12. Stitch along the tuck sewing lines.

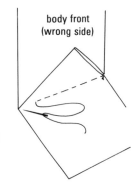

10.12

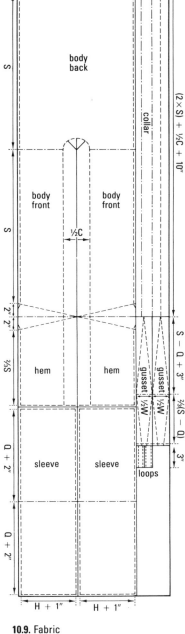

10.9. Fabric

WOMAN'S HAORI PATTERN

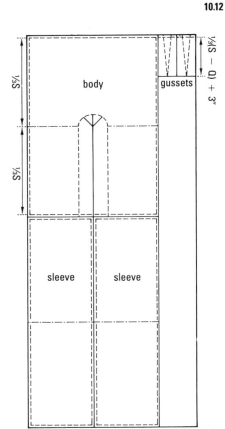

10.10. Lining

Lining same as fabric except where otherwise indicated.

4. Sew the gusset lining piece to the gusset fabric. The lining piece should be long enough to make both halves equal (Fig. 10.13). Follow step 3 for Man's *Haori* (Unlined), except note that the woman's gusset should be sewn to leave a gap between *a* and the point where the sleeve attaches to the body (Fig. 10.14).

5. Stitch lining body piece to fabric hem pieces. Fold lining up into position, wrong side facing wrong side of fabric. Follow steps 9 and 10 for Full Lining. Tuck under raw ends of each gusset and blindstitch closed. Finish off sides above gussets. Figure 10.15 shows the staggered seam line typical of *haori* linings (the garment illustrated is inside out).

6. Sew and attach the loops and collar following steps 1–8 for *Haori* Jacket Collar (p. 38).

Man's Haori (Lined)

A man's lined *haori* is made in basically the same manner as a woman's, except for the tapering at the sides and the lack of an opening under each sleeve.

1. Cut out the pattern pieces for a woman's lined *haori* (Figs. 10.9, 10.10), using measurements derived from Making the Pattern (p. 10). Alter as follows: Substitute measurement B (man's shoulder line) for A (woman's shoulder line) and redraw the side seams to match the tapered lines in Figure 10.4. Be sure to transfer the tapered side seams to the lining pattern as well. Sew in a center back seam.

2. Follow steps 2–6 for Woman's *Haori* (Lined).

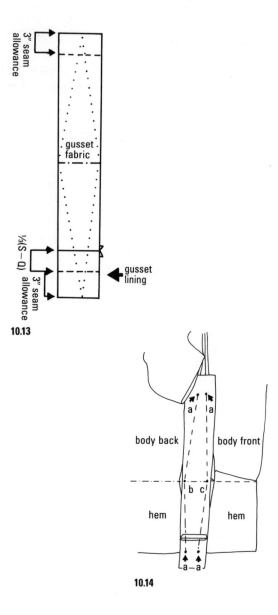

10.13

10.14

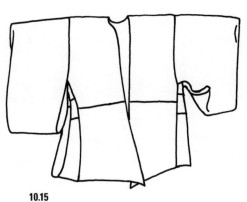

10.15

Woman's Haori (Unlined)

A woman's unlined *haori* is made in basically the same manner as a man's, except for the straight side seams and the gap under each sleeve.

1. Cut out the pattern pieces for a man's unlined *haori* (Fig. 10.4), using measurements derived from Making the Pattern (p. 10). Alter as follows: Substitute measurement A (woman's shoulder line) for B (man's shoulder line) and replace the tapered side seam lines with straight side seams as shown in Figure 10.9. Sew in a center back seam.

2. Follow steps 2–6 for Man's *Haori* (Unlined). Note, however, that the sleeves do not angle in as they do for a man's jacket. Note also that the woman's gusset should be sewn to leave a gap between point *a* and the point where the sleeve attaches to the body (Fig. 10.14).

HAORI JACKET VARIATIONS

1. Jacket with extra width around the bottom of the garment (created by widening the base of each pattern piece), modified sleeves, and a flowing, triangular collar. Shown with *mompe* slacks, *kaku* obi, and a kimono blouse (Kimono Variation 2).

2. *Haori* jacket with a dramatic, wide collar that doubles as a hood.

3. Dress made by eliminating the *haori* collar and stitching the front closed. Has a Nehru collar and gathered boat-bottom sleeves with cuffs.

4. Try wearing a standard *haori* jacket in this unusual way to fashion a self-contained blouse and jacket. The bodice ends are pinned inconspicuously and belted around the waist for added security.

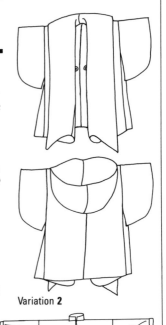

Variation **2**

Variation **3**

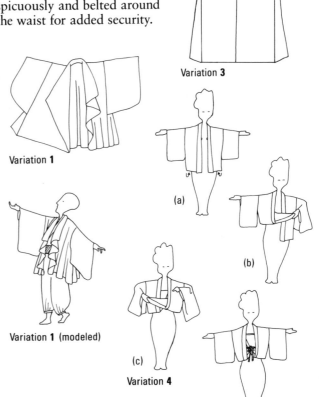

Variation **1**

Variation **1** (modeled)

(a)

(b)

(c)

(d)

Variation **4**

11 Hanten Jacket

This informal jacket (*hanten*) resembles the *haori* jacket in a number of ways. Both are worn over kimono. Since the kimono is closed with an obi tied into a large knot in back, neither jacket is belted, thus keeping the lines smooth and straight. Both jackets are much shorter than regular kimono, and both are worn by either sex.

The difference lies in the construction and purpose of the garments. The *hanten* has no gusset (or side panel) at the side as the *haori* does, and is most often worn as a work jacket, quite often over pants, while the *haori* is considered a formal or semi-formal coat to be worn over kimono only. The informal *hanten* comes in a range of lengths and sleeve shapes so it can be designed to suit the job at hand.

Workmen's *hanten*, usually unlined, have tube sleeves and may be tied closed with a cloth band around the hips. Traditional craftsmen as well as laborers, gardeners, carpenters, fishermen, firemen, and farmers count among those who favor these jackets. A company or family will print its name vertically on both sides of the collar and emblazon its crest on the center back of the jacket. The company name may also be printed in stylized Chinese characters around the bottom hem. Members of the group

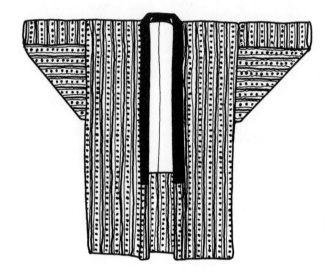

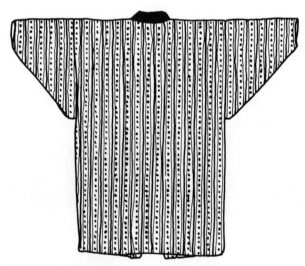

11.1, 11.2. *Hanten* jacket

wear their jackets with pride, the crests and names uniting them. *Hanten* are used in much the same way that Western organizations use printed T-shirts to instill a sense of group identity.

Presented here is a padded jacket with wrapped sleeves (*makisode*; Figs. 11.1, 11.2). This popular style of sleeve is particularly practical for working in and around the house, as the cone-shaped sleeve doesn't get in the way. Each sleeve is formed ingeniously from a rectangle of cloth. Feel free, however, to substitute any of the sleeves shown in Sleeves (p. 29); all except flutter sleeves and long sleeves are commonly used on *hanten* jackets. The length of the finished jacket made here is standard: two-thirds of measurement K (the distance from the base of your neck to the floor). The jacket is padded for extra warmth, resulting in a perfect housecoat for cold climates or a light wrap for outdoors. If you choose not to pad the garment, you may also eliminate the lining.

Materials

A medium-weight cotton woven in stripes of browns or blues is the traditional choice for the wrapped-sleeve *hanten*. A light cotton of chestnut brown or indigo blue is used for the lining. The padding is normally 100% wool batting with *mawata* silk. Even for nontraditional weaves, fabrics with stripes running lengthwise not only are slimming but also show off the wrapped-sleeve design. Guatemalan cotton weaves and upholstery fabric are suitable for a dressier look, while a denim could make this a

jacket to live in. Polyfil batting may be used instead of wool.

Ideas

Make a workman's *hanten* by omitting lining and batting and substituting tube sleeves. For a "happi" coat, shorten the workman's *hanten* and select a festive, brightly colored cotton fabric. Pockets or ties may be added to any of the *hanten*.

INSTRUCTIONS

---

1. Cut out the pattern pieces (Figs. 11.3–6), using measurements derived from Making the Pattern (p. 10). Follow the instructions under Padding (p. 20) as you sew the jacket. Sew a center back seam in lining and fabric body pieces.

2. To make the left sleeve, first sew the lining to the fabric, right sides together, along the wristhole (Fig. 11.7). Clip seam allowance at dot. Open up the layers and iron the seam flat (Fig. 11.8).

3. With right sides of fabric and lining facing up, fold up the bottom inside corners to align with the outer fabric edges (Fig. 11.8).

4. Fold top edge down to overlap by 1″ (Fig. 11.9). Sleeve should appear as in Figure 11.10.

5. Turn the overlapping edges so that right sides of fabric (and lining) face, and sew the edges together, being careful not to catch wristhole seam allowance in stitching (Fig. 11.11). Iron seam open.

6. Lay sleeve and lining flat (Fig. 11.12) and sew along the dotted lines. Fold up corners

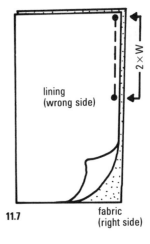

lining (wrong side)

2 × W

fabric (right side)

11.7

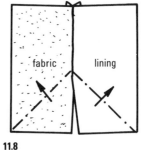

fabric   lining

11.8

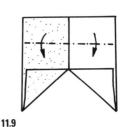

11.9

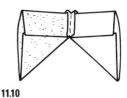

11.10

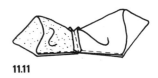

11.11

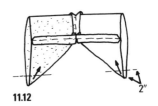

2″

11.12

Hanten Jacket

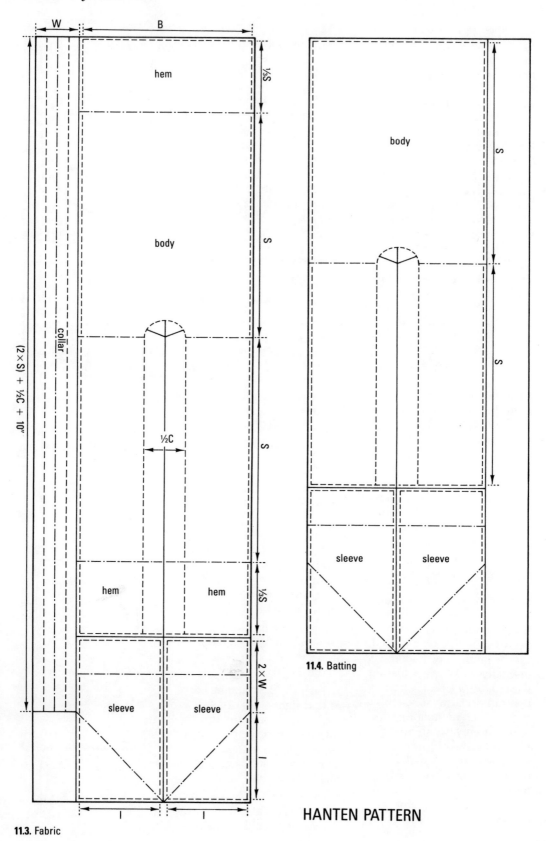

11.3. Fabric

11.4. Batting

HANTEN PATTERN

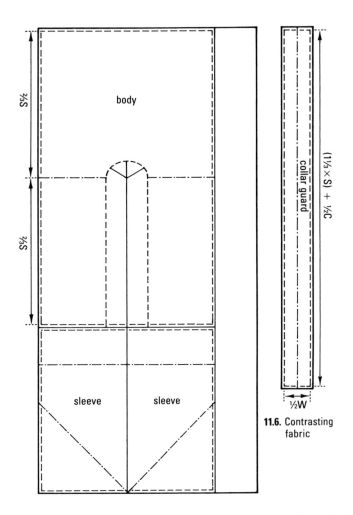

⅔S

⅔S

body

sleeve   sleeve

collar guard

(1⅓ × S) + ½C

½W

11.6. Contrasting fabric

11.5. Lining   *Lining and batting same as fabric except where otherwise indicated.*

along stitching to front of sleeve. To make the right sleeve, follow steps 2–4, but start off with lining fabric on top in Figure 11.7.

7. Sew sleeves to body, right sides of fabric (or lining) together, as shown in Figure 11.13. Be sure the horizontal seams on the sleeves are facing the front side of the garment.

8. With right sides facing, sew the side seams of the body fabric together from lower edge of sleeve to bottom edge of body. Do the same with the lining. Iron the seams open. The garment should appear as in Figure 11.14.

9. Without turning right-side out, arrange the garment so that the body fronts of lining and fabric face each other

(Fig. 11.15). Pin the bottom edge of the lining to the bottom edge of the face fabric, with right sides facing. Sew the bottom edges together from end to end, between dots.

10. Turn the jacket inside out at the neck opening so the fabric is on the outside (Fig. 11.16). Since body lining is shorter than body fabric, fold fabric to lining side at bottom. Align fabric and lining around neck and front opening, and baste through all layers 3⁄8″ from raw edge.

11. Sew on collar (see *Hanten* Jacket or Vest Collar, p. 37) and collar guard (see Collar Guard, p. 42). Figure 11.17 shows finished jacket.

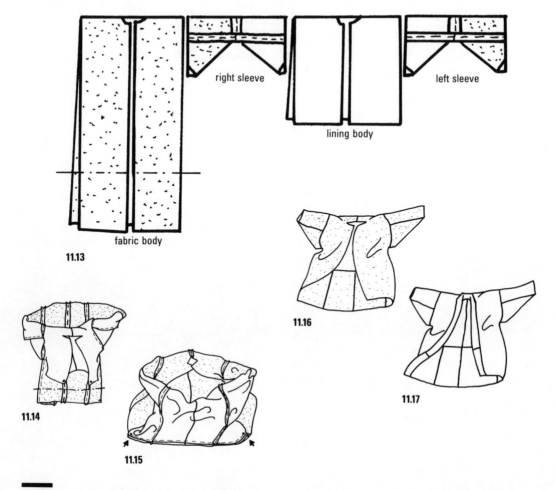

right sleeve

left sleeve

lining body

fabric body

11.13

11.16

11.14

11.17

11.15

HANTEN JACKET VARIATIONS

1. *Hanten* jacket with long sleeves (*nagasode*), a square neckline, and two extra front panels closed with hidden snaps.

2. Coat with a Western collar, a button tab at neck, boat-bottom sleeves, pockets, and a front that closes flush.

3. Short jacket tapered at the waist, with a tie closing, constructed from one piece of fabric plus two front insets.

4. Same as Variation 3, but with front panels that meet, a front zipper closure, a Western collar, and pockets.

5. Gi (garment for wear when practicing judo) decorated with *sashiko* embroidery for added strength. Has square sleeves and wide front panels. Usually worn with a belt.

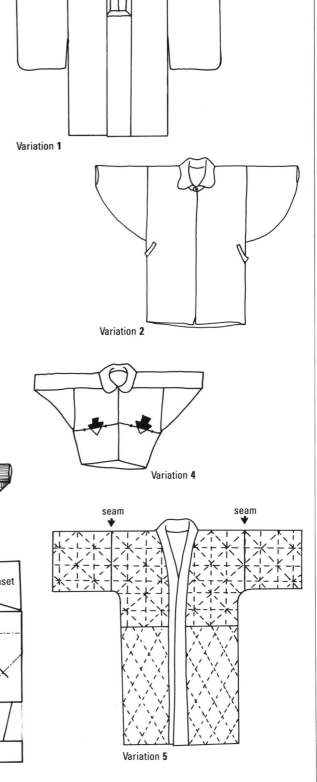

Variation **1**

Variation **2**

Variation **4**

Variation **5**

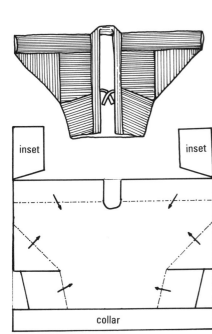

Variation **3** (with pattern layout)

12 Wraparound Tops

No doubt summer in Japan would be unbearable to many Japanese men if they were deprived of their *jimbei* (Figs. 12.1, 12.2). These comfortable, loose wraparound tops are made of light cotton or linen and their side seams are open, connected only by decorative featherstitching, so as to take advantage of any passing breeze. The back may bear a pictorial decoration dyed in the fabric before construction: Fierce samurai, ukiyo-e reproductions, and cartoon characters are popular motifs. The *jimbei* top is considered a very casual, men's summer garment to be worn around the house; on the way to and from the public bath; or for a leisurely stroll around the neighborhood on a Sunday afternoon. Completing the outfit are, typically, matching knee-length shorts and sandals or geta (wooden clogs). To the Western eye, it may seem as if Japanese men parade the streets in their pajamas.

There are probably as many Japanese women who swear by their *hippari* tops (Figs. 12.3, 12.4). Of construction similar to the *jimbei*, except for tapered sleeves that stay out of the way and sewn (closed) side seams, the *hippari* is an infinitely practical as well as attractive top. Although considered a unisex garment, this top is worn primarily by women—over infor-

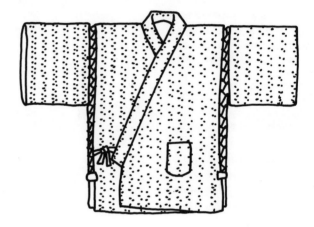

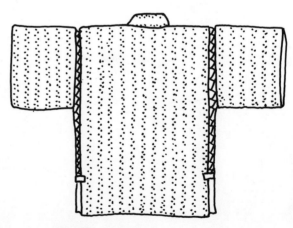

12.1, 12.2. *Jimbei* top

mal kimono around the house, over loose-fitting cotton slacks (*mompe*) for working in the fields, and over jeans for shopping in the neighborhood. Any season is appropriate, with the weight, design, and color of the fabric determining suitability. Unlike the *jimbei*, which is never lined, the *hippari* may be lined and even padded for additional warmth. The *hippari* often has a collar guard (especially when worn over Western clothes), while the *jimbei* does not; the *jimbei*, worn directly against the skin, is laundered frequently instead. Both tops overlap in front and are tied closed at two points, one of which is concealed.

Presented here are a knee-length (unlined) *jimbei* with the typical three-quarters-length tube sleeves and a lined hip-length *hippari* with boat-bottom sleeves closed at the wrist with elastic. Both garments have pockets—the *jimbei* a patch pocket and the *hippari* an inset pocket.

A box pleat has been added to both garments to adapt them to Western body shapes. If your hips (measurement G) are at least 1″ less in circumference than $2 \times B$ (or A), then it is better to omit the box pleat from the pattern and instructions. If $2 \times B$ (or A) is the same as or only slightly larger than your hips, a small box pleat (about 2″–3″) will make the garment more comfortable. Otherwise, add a box pleat that is *at least* as wide as the difference between hip measurement G and $2 \times B$ (or A). See Figure 12.5.

Materials

For *jimbei*, a crisp cotton or linen is traditional, but synthetics and blends may also be

12.3, 12.4. *Hippari* top

used. The featherstitching requires about two skeins (approximately 24 feet) of 6-ply embroidery floss or a comparable weight of crochet thread. Be sure to select a floss, thread, or cord of a weight and ply compatible with the fabric. You may substitute coarse lace tape for the featherstitching, in which case you need a length of lace measuring $(P + Q + 5″) \times 2$, or about 2½ yards for an average figure.

For *hippari*, the season determines the fiber and weight of the fabric. A heavy cotton is the usual choice. Select any lining fabric that suits the face fabric, such as a lightweight cotton or synthetic or china silk. You will need about ½ yard of ½" elastic for the wrist openings if you make the sleeves presented here.

Ideas

Add large pockets! Even just one will make either top more practical. Use a contrasting fabric for collar and sleeves or collar and sleeve linings. Wear the *jimbei* as a bathing suit cover-up. Or, turn the *jimbei* into a formal dress: Lengthen the body, make the garment from satin or silk, featherstitch from the hem to mid-thigh level (or higher) with silk or metallic thread, and use a silk frog or fancy metal closing in place of the tie that shows.

Turn the *hippari* into a coat: Lengthen and line the garment, use a heavy fabric, and close the front overlap with a large button or other sturdy clasp (see variations at end of project). The *hippari*, with the addition of a roomy pocket or two, has already been adopted as a work smock by some day-care workers, teachers, and hospitals in America.

INSTRUCTIONS

Jimbei Top

1. Cut out the pattern pieces (Fig. 12.5), using measurements derived from Making the Pattern (p. 10).

2. Press all fabric edges of body and sleeves under ¼" to wrong side except for neck opening. Fold all edges under another ¼" except for neck opening and bottom of

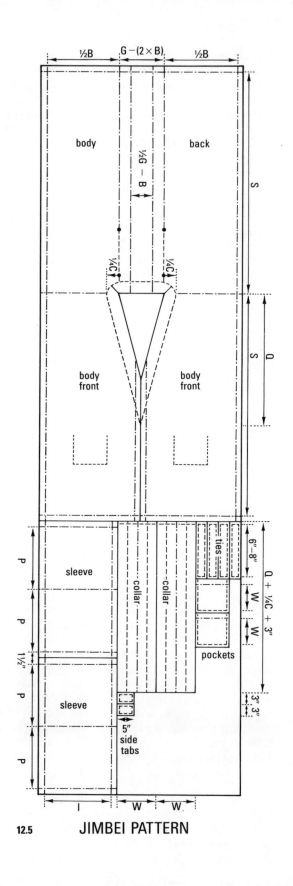

12.5   **JIMBEI PATTERN**

sleeves. Topstitch edges in place by hand or machine (Fig. 12.6), sewing bottom edges of body last.

3. Lay the body and sleeves out flat, wrong-side up, aligning center point of each sleeve with center point (shoulder line) of body. Starting at the center point, use a measuring tape or ruler to measure ½″ intervals along the entire sleeve edge and along the body edge to a point 4″–5″ below the waistline (Fig. 12.7). Note how intervals are staggered. On the wrong side of the garment, mark intervals with tailor's chalk ¼″ in from the hemmed edges.

4. Thread a sharp needle with enough embroidery floss to stitch the entire side seam without stopping; three times the length of the body piece from back bottom to front bottom (i.e. 6 × S) should be enough. Featherstitch the sleeve to the body (Fig. 12.8), and then the body sides together. Start stitching ¾″ from the bottom front edge of the sleeve and stop about ¾″ from the other edge; pause to sew the sleeve bottom seam (turn the sleeve inside out and, with right sides together, sew the bottom edge together ½″ from the folded edge); and then continue featherstitching the side seam. When finished, knot thread on the wrong side of the body back. Alternatively, you can join the seams with the Seven Treasures stitch (see box), with readymade coarse lace (Fig. 12.9), or with other forms of faggoting. Finished featherstitching should appear as in Figure 12.10.

5. Fold each side tab piece in half and sew ½″ from the long raw edge. Turn each tube inside out, tuck in the raw

edges at the ends, and slip-stitch closed. Press flat. Top-stitch the tabs across the side seams at a point 4″–5″ below the waistline, covering the end of the featherstitching (Fig. 12.10). These pieces help keep the featherstitching from pulling out.

6. To make the box pleat, stitch along the sewing lines of the center of the body back, right sides together, beginning at the neck. Stop at a point that corresponds to the bottom of measurement N on your size chart or a drop of 3″–8″ from the collar. Iron the short pleat flat and blindstitch the edges down (Fig. 12.11).

7. Right sides facing, sew together the two collar pieces along one short end to make one long collar strip. Attach the collar following steps 3–6 of *Hanten* Jacket or Vest Collar (p. 37). Note that the collar does not extend to bottom front edge of garment.

8. Prepare the four tie pieces as you did the side reinforcements (sew into tubes, turn right-side out, and blindstitch the ends; see step 5). Attach the ties at waist level at the four points shown in Figure 12.12. Note that for both men's and women's garments in Japan, the front closes left over right.

9. Turn each sleeve inside out and press the bottom seam open, preserving the ¼″ fold pressed in earlier, and blindstitch seam allowance to sleeve (Fig. 12.13).

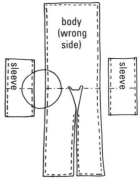

12.6

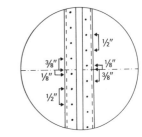

12.7

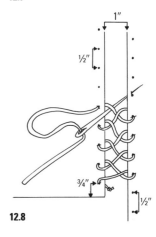

12.8

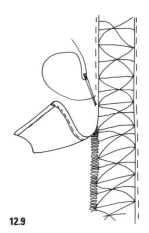

12.9

10. To make patch pockets, press under all edges of each pocket piece ¼″ to the wrong side. Press under the top edge of each pocket another ¼″ and topstitch to finish off. Position each pocket, where comfortable, on a front body panel and topstitch in place around the other three sides of the pocket.

Hippari Top

1. Cut out the pattern pieces (Figs. 12.14, 12.15), using measurements derived from Making the Pattern (p. 10). If you are not adding a box pleat, sew in a center back seam, taking a ½″ seam allowance, in both fabric and lining.

2. Sew inset pockets in place on front panels; follow any standard instructions using the pocket lining pieces and fabric welt pieces provided here. Alternatively, add patch pockets following step 10 of *Jimbei* Top.

3. To make boat-bottom sleeves, follow steps 2–5 under Full Lining (p. 25), using Figures 5.23 and 5.24 as a guide. You may wish to attach the sleeve to the body along its full width as shown in Figures 12.3 and 12.4. Trim seam allowance at wrist to ¼″.

4. Sew in a casing at each wrist by topstitching ¾″ from the seam. Carefully rip out the sleeve-bottom seam on the lining side between wrist edge and topstitching (Fig. 12.16). Thread a piece of elastic— enough for a comfortable fit— through the casing and stitch the ends together securely (Fig. 12.17). Blindstitch the casing opening closed (Fig. 12.18).

5. Sew the fabric side seams together, with right sides facing, from the bottom of the sleeve to a point about crotch level, or several inches below the waist. Iron the side seams

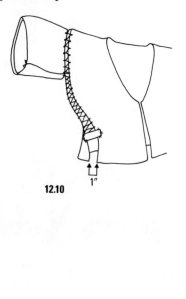

12.10

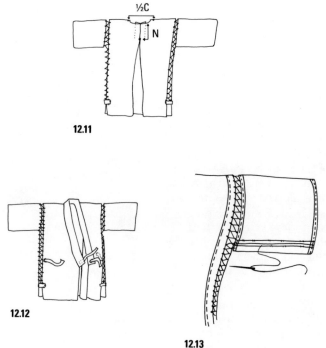

12.11

12.12

12.13

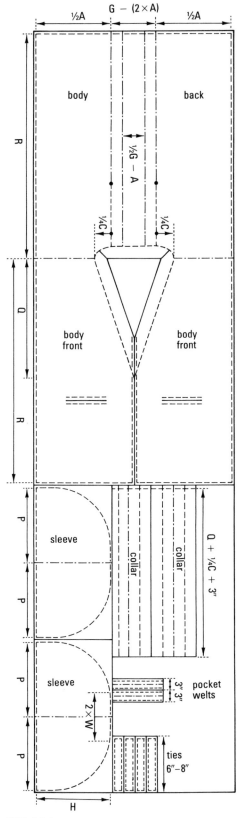

12.14. Fabric

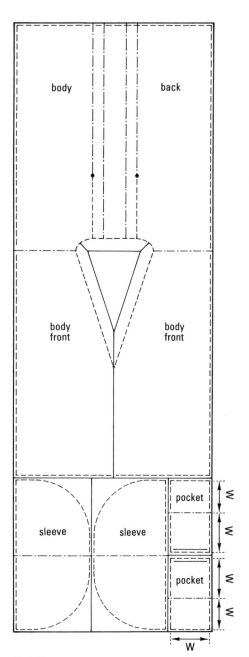

12.15. Lining

HIPPARI PATTERN

*Lining same as fabric except
where otherwise indicated.*

open. Repeat for lining. Sew lining to body, right sides together, along the hem as in Figure 12.19. Turn bottom hem edge of garment right-side out. Continue with steps 9 and 10 of Full Lining.

6. Follow steps 6–8 of *Jimbei* Top.

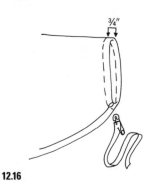

12.16

12.17

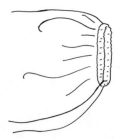

12.18

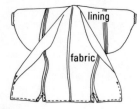

12.19

SEVEN TREASURES STITCH

This attractive stitch is sometimes seen on *jimbei* tops, but it may be used to add a decorative touch to any garment. Be sure to finish off the fabric edges first unless you are joining selvedges. These instructions are tailored to the *jimbei*, but the principles apply to other uses.

1. Follow step 3 for *Jimbei* Top, except do not stagger the ½" intervals—align the marks on the opposing fabric edges. Stitch a loose blanketstitch along each garment edge, leaving a loop between stitches (Fig. 1).

2. Thread two needles and weave them in and out of the stitching, making square knots as shown in Figure 2. The needles will not penetrate the fabric except at the beginning and end of the stitching, when you knot the thread. Darning needles are recommended. Start at each front sleeve bottom and sew in the same manner as for featherstitching. Finish off by knotting the thread on the reverse side of the fabric.

3. Figure 3 shows finished Seven Treasures stitching.

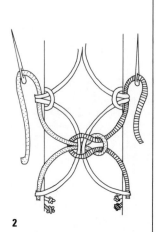

2

3

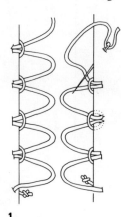

1

WRAPAROUND TOP VARIATIONS

1. Traditional woman's rain-coat (*uwappari*). Follow the basic *hippari* pattern but lengthen the hem, substitute Genroku sleeves, add a button closure, and alter the neckline.

2. Ankle-length robe with side gussets added for fullness. Based on the *hippari* pattern.

3. Short top with chiseled sleeves (*sogisode*) and a box pleat added at the small of the back for a more tailored look. This design, based on the *hippari*, is especially suited to large-busted or small-waisted women.

4. Cocktail dress based on the *jimbei* pattern, but with a sculpted collar, boat-bottom sleeves, and a belt instead of ties.

Variation **1**

Variation **2**

Variation **3**

Variation **3** (rear view)

Variation **4**

13 Vests

Traditional vests (*chan-chanko*) are associated with children in Japan, but adults also wear them for their utility and warmth. Padded with batting, as they usually are in Japan, these vests provide warmth while allowing free movement of the arms. In this respect, they compare favorably to down vests.

Presented here are two styles of vest: a traditional pattern (Figs. 13.1, 13.2), most easily made with narrow Japanese fabric (about 14″ wide), and a modern adaptation (Figs. 13.3, 13.4), which is more suitable for wider widths of fabric. Both vests hit the body right below the buttocks, but you can adjust the length of the body piece to make either vest shorter (Q) or longer (R).

Materials

Medium-weight cotton, flat-weave silk, and wool challis have been the traditional choices for the outer fabric. Lightweight cotton or silk was usually used for the lining, and 100% wool batting in combination with *mawata* silk was the padding.

Other suggested fabrics include slub silks, textured cottons, polyester blends, tapestry weaves (e.g., old Kilim rugs), and upholstery fabrics. Polyfil batting may be substituted for the traditional wool.

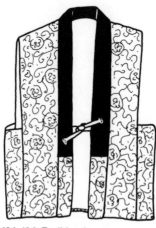 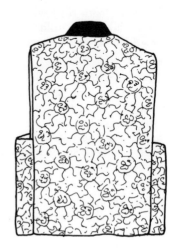

13.1, 13.2. Traditional vest

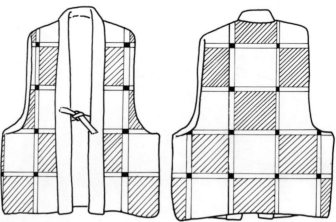

13.3, 13.4. Modern vest

Note that if heavy outer fabric is used, adding batting may make the vest too bulky.

Ideas

To transform this everyday garment into part of an elegant evening ensemble, hand-dye silk for the outer fabric and *sashiko*-embroider the finished padded silk vest with silk thread. For carefree travel or for purse-free living, add pockets with zipper or velcro closings on the inside for storing money, traveler's checks, passports, and the like. Design the pockets to suit your own needs.

INSTRUCTIONS

Traditional Vest

1. Cut out the pattern pieces (Figs. 13.5–8), using measurements derived from Making the Pattern (p. 10). Dimensions for lining and batting pattern pieces are the same as the corresponding outer fabric pieces. Read Padding (p. 20) before proceeding.

2. Sew in darts at the shoulders as indicated by the dotted lines on the pattern. The size of the dart depends on the slope of your shoulders. Generally, a 1″–2″ drop is enough. If you have narrow or sloping shoulders, more may be required. If you have very broad or square shoulders, you may need less or none at all. Make darts in both the outer fabric and the lining.

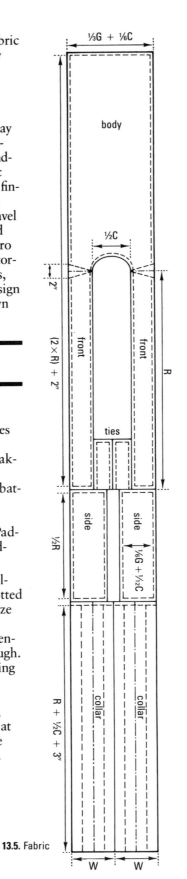

13.5. Fabric

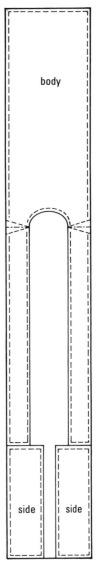

13.6. Lining

Dimensions same as fabric except where otherwise indicated.

TRADITIONAL VEST PATTERN

Vests

3. Right sides together, sew lining side panels to fabric side pieces along short ends (Fig. 13.9). Turn right-side out.

4. Pin fabric body to lining body, with right sides together. Sew together at bottom front and bottom back edges. Leave inside out. At this point the garment should appear as in Figure 13.10.

5. Insert one of the side panels between the fabric and lining at the bottom back of the body piece. Position it so the fabric of the side piece faces the fabric (not lining) of the body. Starting at the bottom edge of the body back, sew the pieces together between the dots shown in Figure 13.11. Repeat for the other side panel.

13.9

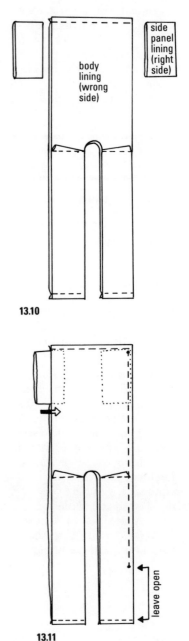

body lining (wrong side)

side panel lining (right side)

13.10

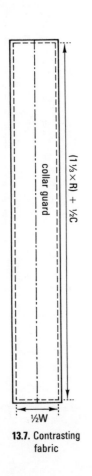

collar guard

$(1\frac{1}{3} \times R) + \frac{1}{2}C$

½W

13.7. Contrasting fabric

body

tie

tie

side

side

13.8. Batting

leave open

13.11

6. Turn the two side panels and the body back right-side out by pulling them through the neck opening (Fig. 13.12). Do not turn the front panels right-side out yet.

7. Insert the unsewn edge of one side panel between the lining and fabric of the corresponding side of the body front. Again, be sure that the fabric of the side panel faces the fabric of the body front, and that the lining sides are facing. Sew the panel in position as shown in Figure 13.13. Repeat for the other panel. Finish turning the garment right-side out. Iron open all seams.

8. Beginning at the bottom front, hand- or machine-baste around the front opening and neck line through the fabric, batting, and lining (Fig. 13.14).

9. Cut some cording or yarn into two pieces, each twice as long as a tie piece. Lay a piece of cord on a scrap of batting measuring 3″ × 8″ (Fig. 13.15). Roll the batting around the cord and tie securely with thread about ¼″ from the edge of the batting (Fig. 13.16).

10. Lay the section of exposed cording on the center of the tie fabric (Fig. 13.17). Fold the tie in half lengthwise over the cord, right sides together. Sew through both fabric layers and the cord, leaving a ¼″ seam allowance (Fig. 13.18). Continue stitching around the long side, being careful not to catch the cord as you go.

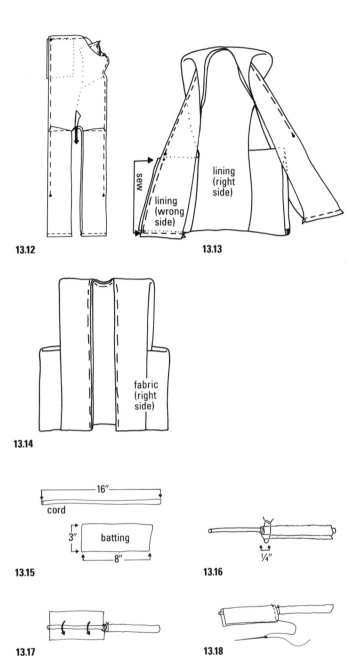

13.12

13.13

13.14

13.15

13.16

13.17

13.18

11. Gently pull the end of the cord protruding from the tie, turning the tie right-side out (Fig. 13.19). Cut off any excess cording or batting extending from either end (Fig. 13.20). Using the other piece of cord from step 9, repeat steps 9–11 to make the other tie.

12. Pin each tie to a front panel, aligning raw edges and with sewn edge of tie facing down (Fig. 13.21). The tie is usually positioned at a point about halfway between the bottom of your rib cage and your navel, but place it where it feels comfortable to you. Tack down the ties.

13. Follow directions for *Hanten* Jacket or Vest Collar (p. 37) to attach the collar. You may want to sew on a dark-color collar guard (p. 42). Besides protecting the garment, it adds a nice accent.

Modern Vest

1. Follow steps 1 and 2 for Traditional Vest, except cut out the pattern pieces in Figures 13.22–25.

2. With right sides together, sew the fabric to the lining along the bottom front and bottom back edges, and around the armhole openings (Fig. 13.26). Turn only the back panel right-side out.

3. Sandwich each back panel side between the lining and fabric of the corresponding front panel side (Fig. 13.27) and sew the sides together through all layers. Turn the whole vest right-side out and press all seams.

4. Follow steps 8–13 for Traditional Vest.

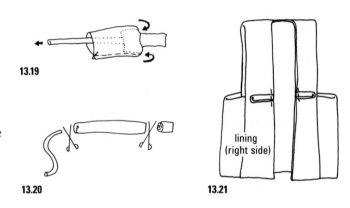

13.19

13.20

13.21

lining (right side)

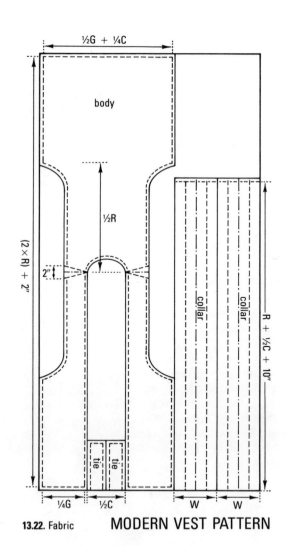

½G + ¼C

body

½R

(2 × R) + 2"

2"

¼G

½C

tie

tie

collar

collar

R + ½C + 10"

W

W

13.22. Fabric

MODERN VEST PATTERN

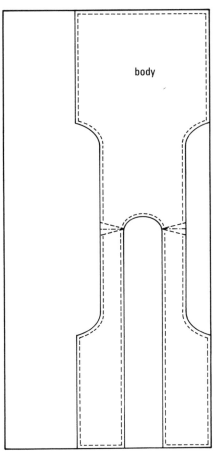

13.23. Lining

Dimensions same as fabric except where otherwise indicated.

$(1\frac{1}{3} \times R) + \frac{1}{2}C$

collar guard

$\frac{1}{2}W$

13.24. Contrasting fabric

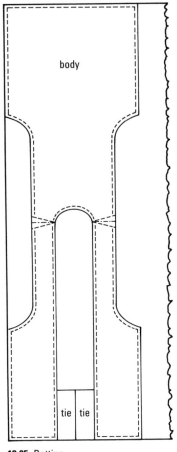

tie tie

13.25. Batting

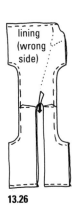

lining (wrong side)

13.26

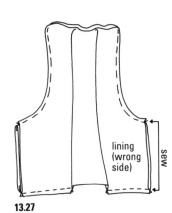

lining (wrong side)

sew

13.27

VEST VARIATIONS

To fashion a jacket from Variations 1, 3, or 4, just add full-length sleeves with cuffs.

1. Traditional vest with a slightly raised side panel. This style is especially suited to people with broad hips. Position the bottom of the side panel so it hits just below waist level.

2. Modern vest with raised sides. The effect is the same as for Variation 1.

3. Same as Variation 2, but with capped sleeves added. To make the sleeve, fold a small square of fabric in half diagonally, right sides out, and sew the two short sides of the triangle to the body, matching the corner of the triangle to the shoulder line.

4. Modern vest with extended and padded shoulders, raised sides, and a shortened collar. In place of ties, small loops (see *Haori* Jacket) have been added to support a small chain with S hooks at either end.

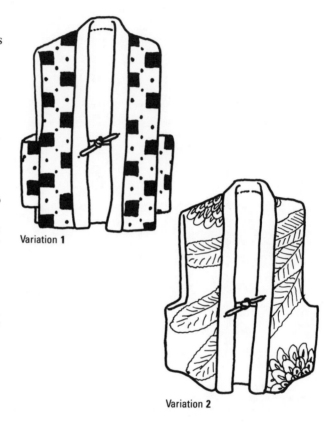

Variation **1**

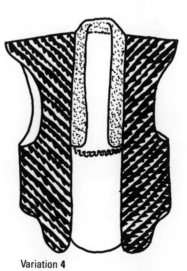

Variation **2**

Variation **3**

Variation **4**

14 Slacks

These loose-fitting slacks
(*mompe*) are most often worn
by female agricultural workers
in modern-day Japan. During
World War II, however, it was
quite common for all women
to wear *mompe*: They were
part of the "uniform" worn
by civilian women's neighborhood battalions. In more
recent times, designers have
brought these slacks into the
realm of high fashion.

Made of cotton, typically
with stripes or indigo-and-
white ikat (*kasuri*) patterns,
these roomy slacks are
designed to be pulled over a
kimono or worn with a *hippari* top tucked into the waist.
The low crotch, three-quarters
length, and elastic waist and
cuffs make them ideal for gardening, bicycling, and other
active wear.

Presented here are two
styles: slacks with elasticized
waist and leg bottoms (Fig.
14.1) and the same basic
slacks with ties at the waist
and bands at the leg bottoms
(Fig. 14.2). The ties are tied in
a simple knot or bow as
shown in Variation 1. Neither
style is lined.

Mompe extend to anywhere
from just below the knee to
mid-calf. These patterns are
for three-quarters-length
slacks, but feel free to adjust
the length to your liking. Similarly, the length and width of
the ties is a matter of preference. At a minimum, make

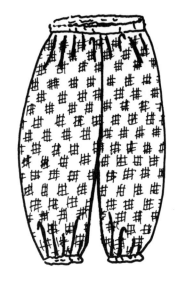

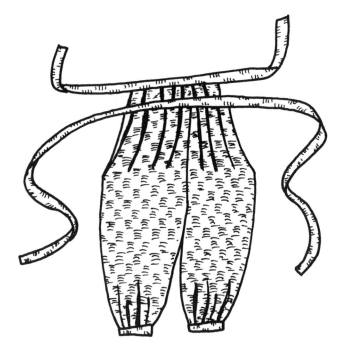

14.1, 14.2. *Mompe* (slacks)

the back tie long enough to reach around your waist to the front and have enough left over to tie a simple knot (say, E + 16″). The front tie should be long enough to wrap around the back and again to the front with enough left over to tie a knot (say, [E × 2] + 16″). Both ties are tied in front.

Materials

Light or medium-weight cotton ikat is the traditional choice of fabric. For the slacks with elasticized waist, you need enough ½″ width elastic to go around your waist and each calf plus about 3″ extra for each piece.

Rough, nubby fabrics such as tussah silk will create a rustic, folksy look, whereas satin or charmeuse can transform the slacks into elegant evening wear.

Ideas

Try wearing the slacks with a kimono blouse (Kimono Variation 2, p. 50) and tied with a *kaku* obi, or with an oversized shirt and a bright red sash tied a little off-center in front. Or make a built-in obi by quadrupling the width of (only) the front tie.

INSTRUCTIONS

Slacks with Elastic Closing

1. Cut out the pattern pieces (Fig. 14.3), using measurements derived from Making the Pattern (p. 10).

2. Sew the two front pieces together, right sides facing, from waist to crotch (Fig. 14.4).

3. Sew the two back pieces together, right sides facing, from waist to crotch (Fig. 14.5).

4. Sew the back to the front along the inseam, right sides facing, beginning at the crotch and sewing toward the bottom of each leg (Fig. 14.6).

5. With right sides of fabric facing, sew the side seams (Fig. 14.7).

6. To make casings at waist and ankles, first press the raw fabric edge ¼″ to the wrong side and fold over another ⅝″ to the wrong side. Topstitch each casing in place, leaving an opening through which to thread the elastic. Thread the elastic pieces through the casings using a safety pin to help guide them along (Fig. 14.8). Stitch the ends of the elastic pieces together after checking the comfort of the fit. Remove safety pins and trim off any excess elastic. Blindstitch the casing openings closed.

Slacks with Tie Closing

1. Follow steps 1–4 for Slacks with Elastic Closing, using the patterns in Figures 14.3 and 14.9.

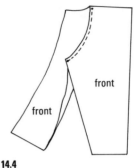

14.4

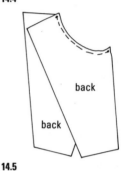

14.5

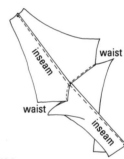

14.6

14.7

14.8

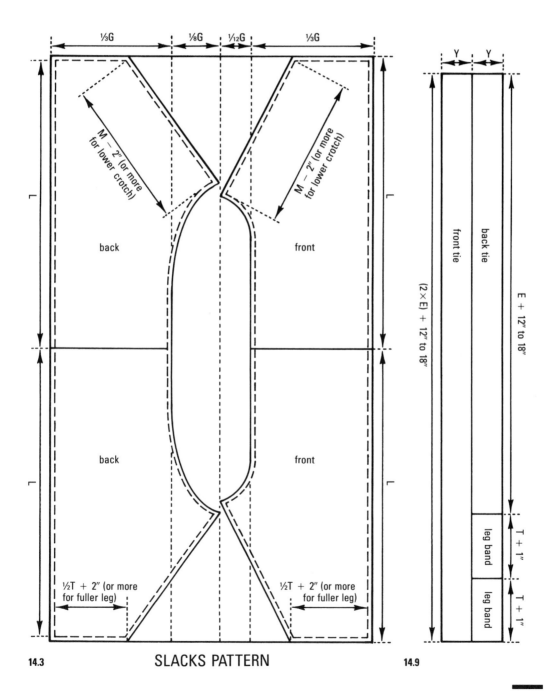

14.3   SLACKS PATTERN   **14.9**

2. With right sides of fabric facing, sew the side seams together beginning at the leg bottom and stopping about 6"–8" from the waist (Fig. 14.10).

3. Roll the unsewn top portion of each side piece to the wrong side, and finish off the edge with a blindstitch (Fig. 14.11).

4. Gather the front at the waist, ⅛" inside the seam line, to reduce the width to a little less than half your waist measurement (E). You may make small pleats (Fig. 14.12) or baste several rows of stitching and pull the threads to gather evenly. Do the same to the back. Staystitch ⅛" inside the seamline of both front and back.

5. Fold and press the front and back waist ties in half lengthwise, wrong sides together. Fold the raw edges to the center fold line, wrong sides together, and press.

6. Match the center points of the ties to the center seams of the front and back, sandwiching the waist edges between the ties (Fig. 14.13). Pin in place. Beginning at the center front, topstitch through all layers to one end of the front tie. Start back at the center front and topstitch to the opposite end. Repeat for the back tie. Tuck unfinished ends of ties in and slipstitch closed.

7. Fold the ankle bands in half lengthwise and in half again as for ties. Press in folds. Baste as for waist to gather the leg bottoms so they will be comfortably snug around your leg, but not so tight you can't easily slip your foot through when putting on the slacks. Pin the ankle bands to the leg bottoms, sandwiching the gathered edges between the bands. Beginning at the outside seam, topstitch through all layers around each leg bottom about ⅛" from top of band edge (Fig. 14.13). Blindstitch closed the opening where band ends meet.

14.10

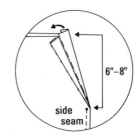

14.11

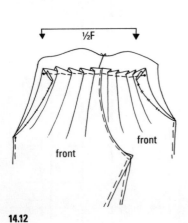

14.12

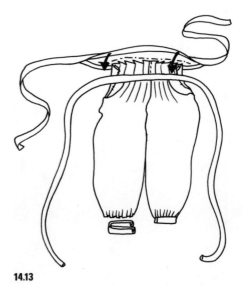

14.13

SLACKS VARIATIONS

1. Slacks with pockets added, shown modeled with a kimono blouse. Snaps hold the pockets in position when worn.

2. Slacks with elasticized waist and lengthened and ungathered leg bottoms.

3. Beach shorts, shown modeled with a *jimbei* top. To make, shorten the slacks that have an elastic closing.

4. Slacks with pockets and a button closing in the shortened ties. Back ties button in front, front ties button in back.

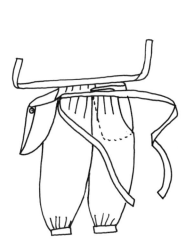

Variation **1**

Variation **1** (modeled)

Variation **2**

Variation **3**

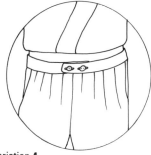

Variation **4**

15 Obi Sashes

帯

The obi, or sash, is the central decorative feature of most Japanese outfits. A wide 13-foot-long woman's obi sewn from a beautiful brocade may be the most expensive part of a kimono ensemble. Some cost many thousands of dollars.

Obi have taken a variety of shapes through the ages. Traditional lore has it that all obi were originally tubular and very short, just long enough to allow one simple half-hitch tie in front. This design, however, proved inconvenient in emergencies. During the Heian period (794–1185), when Kyoto was plagued with a series of fires, it is said that many women lost their expensive, elaborately woven ties—they fell off as the women fled their homes in panic.

Perhaps that is one reason why obi became longer, enabling more elaborate and secure knots. In their heyday, the seventeenth to the mid-nineteenth centuries, obi were tied in scores of different bows and knots bearing such names as Nesting Sparrow and Butterfly Spirit. The wearer's age, social status, profession, and even mood were reflected in her choice of obi and knot.

While the obi once functioned alone to hold a kimono closed, today a series of smaller cords does the actual work of holding the kimono layers in place. The decorative obi is used primarily to hide

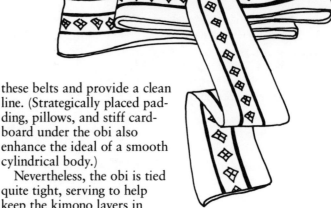

15.1. *Kaku* obi

these belts and provide a clean line. (Strategically placed padding, pillows, and stiff cardboard under the obi also enhance the ideal of a smooth cylindrical body.)

Nevertheless, the obi is tied quite tight, serving to help keep the kimono layers in place as well as to keep the bow or knot from coming untied. For nontraditional wear, tie the obi to a comfortable tightness, though it shouldn't be so loose that it will come undone.

The standard obi consists of three parts. The *do-mawari* (girth) is the central portion that wraps twice around the waist. This portion varies in length from person to person, depending on the waist measurement. Waist measurements should take into account the clothing to be worn under the obi; for women wearing kimono Japanese style, this means using the *padded* waist measurement.

The *te* ("hand") is the short (24") end that is usually used to finish off the knot. The *otaiko* ("drum") is the long (45") end used to form the

15.2. *Maru* obi

bow loops. The *te* and *otaiko* don't vary in length because the size of the bow doesn't normally change. (Extremely tall or heavy people, however, may wish to increase these two measurements by 5"–10" in order to tie a larger, more proportional knot.) In Japan, because there has been so little variation in body sizes until modern times, obi are often sold in a standard, one-size-fits-all length.

There are several distinct types of obi. Women wear wide obi (*maru* obi, *fukuro* obi, and Nagoya obi) as well as narrower sashes (*hanhaba* obi and *hoso* obi). Men wear the narrow *kaku* obi and the casual *heko* obi. Both sexes may wear a simple everyday obi of moderate width that is coarsely woven from cotton, silk, or linen to the appropriate length. A common variety, the *sakiori* ("woven from scraps") obi, is woven from strips of shredded old clothing.

The *maru* ("round") obi is worn on very formal occasions, such as weddings and Coming-of-Age ceremonies. It is usually sewn from a brocade, often woven with scattered strands of gold thread. This obi is folded in half lengthwise before being wrapped around the waist. Most Japanese *maru* obi are about 13 feet long and are constructed of a double layer of the same high-quality fabric.

Some Japanese adapt this principle to make their own inexpensive obi for home wear. They piece together an obi from scraps, using nicer fabric for the ends and any remnants for the part that will be hidden. The only caution: You must tie a knot that will conceal the undecorated portion (for traditional wear), or make sure the undecorated portion will provide a pleasing effect if it shows (for nontraditional wear).

The *kaku* ("square") obi, for men, is constructed in the same manner as, but to somewhat smaller dimensions than, the *maru* obi.

Presented here are instructions for making and knotting a *kaku* obi (Fig. 15.1). Although worn only by men in Japan, it is presented here as a practical choice for nontraditional wear by both sexes: The relatively narrow width makes it comfortable and the shell knot is both compact and easy to tie. With slight modifications, a *maru* obi (Fig. 15.2) may be constructed using the directions for *kaku* obi.

For more ties or instructions on wearing obi with kimono in the traditional manner, see *The Book of Kimono* listed in Appendix 3.

Obi Sashes

Materials

Because a heavy interfacing is used, a wide variety of fabric weights may be used for *kaku* or *maru* obi. Popular choices are flat-weaves, brocades, and striped or patterned silks, cottons, and synthetics. As a general rule, silk will hold a knot better. Do not use a fabric with much give to the weave, as it will tend to pucker and stretch out with use. For interfacing, use heavy cotton duck or sailcloth, or coarse horsehair or linen interfacing.

For tying obi on yourself, clips come in handy. Those used to close potato-chip bags (one brand is "chip clip") are especially useful, as they are long and the rubber grippers won't damage the fabric.

Ideas

Just as a belt can transform an outfit, so too can an obi transform either Western or Japanese wear. The wider *maru* obi lends itself to surface decoration—dyeing, embroidery, patchwork, appliqué, the display of brooches, buttons, or pins, and so on. You might try combining an obi with narrow cords, belts, or scarves in novel ways.

Feel free not to follow traditional tying instructions slavishly; the infinite variety of Japanese knots is no doubt the result of individual experimentation. Some knots work nicely with non-obi sashes, such as the Andean strap pictured on p. 66, or for other applications, such as decorative packaging.

While virtually all obi knots are positioned in the back in modern-day Japan, try off-center placement in front for a stylish nontraditional look, such as that pictured on p. 59. (In past centuries, the Japanese also tied obi in front.)

INSTRUCTIONS

Kaku Obi

1. Prewash the fabric and iron out any stretch in the weave, going with the grain and taking care not to iron in puckers. Determine your

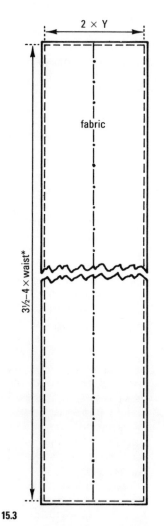
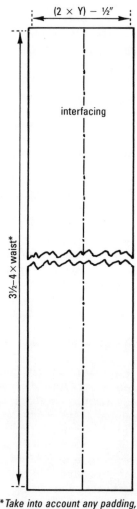

15.3

KAKU OBI PATTERN

Take into account any padding, clothing, and the obi's position on body when measuring.

measurements and cut out the pattern (Fig. 15.3). For the obi's length, thin people should opt for 4 × waist, heavier people should choose 3½ × waist. Do not use the selvedge of the fabric as a pattern piece edge, or be sure to cut it off before measuring.

2. Fold the fabric in half lengthwise, right sides together, and sew between the dots (Figs. 15.4, 15.5).

3. Turn the obi right-side out, and press (Fig. 15.6).

4. Fold the interfacing lengthwise so that the edges are staggered ½″ (Fig. 15.7). Press. Staggering the edges keeps the total obi thickness from getting too bulky.

5. Fashion a stiff "threader" from cardboard and sew or pin it to the interfacing (Fig. 15.8). This threader serves the same function as a safety pin used in threading elastic through a casing. Poke a hole in the narrow end of the cardboard and attach a cord as long as the obi or longer.

Reach through one end of the obi and grasp the end of the cord. Pull the cord through (Fig. 15.9), keeping the obi pulled taut while threading the interfacing into position. This is easiest done with the help of a friend (Fig. 15.10). Make sure the folded edges of fabric and interfacing are aligned. The wider half of the interfacing should lie behind the fabric seam allowance (Fig. 15.11).

6. Fold under the raw fabric edges and slipstitch closed (Figs. 15.11, 15.12).

7. To wear, tie in a shell knot. To store, see folding instructions in chapter 18.

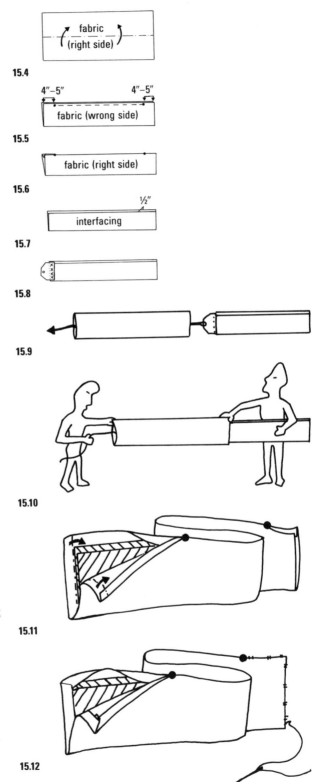

15.4

15.5

15.6

15.7

15.8

15.9

15.10

15.11

15.12

Obi Sashes

Maru Obi

For this woman's obi, follow the directions for *kaku* obi (a man's obi), except alter the dimensions of the pattern pieces as shown in Figure 15.13.

To wear, tie in an *otaiko*, or drum, knot (see *The Book of Kimono*) or experiment on your own. To store, see folding instructions in chapter 18.

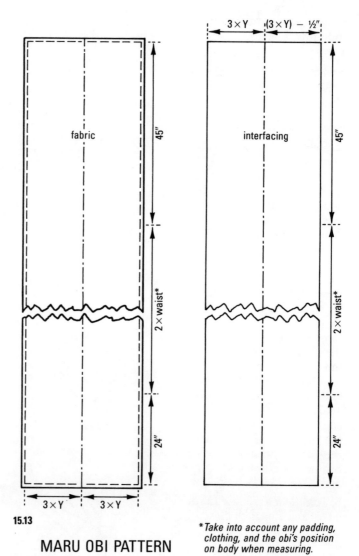

15.13

MARU OBI PATTERN

*Take into account any padding, clothing, and the obi's position on body when measuring.

SHELL KNOT

The shell (*kai no kuchi*) knot, used by men in Japan, is designed for the *kaku* obi. Tie it in front, where you can see what you're doing, then shift the knot into position—slightly off-center in back—by rotating the entire obi around your waist. Remember that men usually wear the obi slung low, somewhere between the waist and hips.

1. Start off by folding the obi in half lengthwise along one end for a distance of about 5 hands (measurement W). Mark this point with a paper clip and position the clip at your center front (Fig. 1).

2. Wrap the other end of the obi twice around the body to look like Figure 2.

3. Fold the long end back on itself (Fig. 2). The amount that gets folded back is deter-mined by your girth, and by trial and error. Start out with 2 to 3 × W. Notice how much of the wider end protrudes from the knot in Figure 6. If too much protrudes when you reach Figures 5 and 6, come back to this step and retie after folding more in. If not enough protrudes, fold less in.

4. Tie a simple half hitch (Fig. 2) and remove clip. Fold the bottom end up (Fig. 3).

5. Bring the upper end down (Fig. 4) and tie a half hitch to form a completed square knot (Fig. 5).

6. Rotate the obi clockwise to the back, positioning it slightly off-center (Fig. 6). For nontraditional wear, you might prefer to position the knot in front. A small pouch (no deeper than the obi is wide) may be pinned between the layers to serve as a purse or pocket.

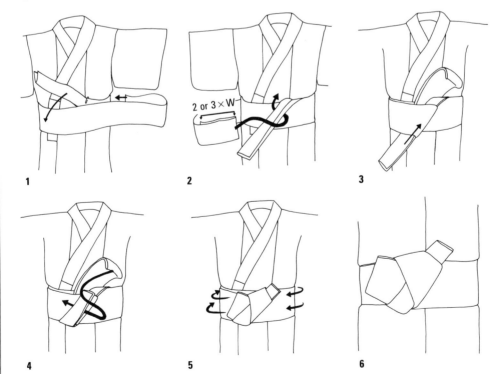

1

2 or 3 × W

2

3

4

5

6

16 Tabi Socks

足袋

Tabi are the two-toed cloth foot coverings that are worn in Japan as we wear socks (Figs. 16.1–3). In ancient times, *tabi*—or to be more accurate, *shitauzu* (the toes weren't split)—were worn only by the upper class. These precursors to *tabi* were made originally from leather and later from silk. Warriors wore *shitauzu* of dyed leather. Commoners went barefoot or sockless under their straw sandals and snowboots.

During the 1500s, as cotton became more widely used, all social classes came to wear the split-toed *tabi*. The split enabled wear with sandals and geta (wooden clogs). In the Edo period (1600–1868), *tabi* reached their peak of development: A variety of styles were created to suit a range of occupations, and a rainbow of colors and patterns were used to indicate the wearer's rank and status.

In modern times, men wear black or navy blue cotton *tabi* around the house while women wear only white. For formal occasions, both sexes wear white cotton *tabi*. Colored or patterned ones are worn by dancers and performers. A popular alternative to *tabi* for casual, daily wear is two-toed knit socks, a thinner version of which are frequently worn under a cousin of the *tabi*, the mid-calf-length *jika-tabi*.

The *jika-tabi* is worn by carpenters, gardeners, and other workers. These tall, rubber-soled *tabi* of sturdy cloth are perfect for catwalking, "ninja feats," and other tasks that require a lightweight, nonbinding "shoe" with good grip.

Construction of a *tabi* is not difficult. There are three pieces of fabric (and lining)—the outpiece that covers the outside of your foot, the inpiece that covers the inside of your foot, and the bottom, or sole, piece. You also need three or more *kohaze*, the small aluminum tabs that hook through thread loops to close the *tabi* along the heel.

While construction is fairly straightforward, adjusting the fit is tricky enough to keep professional *tabi* makers well employed in Japan. The proper fit of a *tabi* is quite snug (most Westerners would call it very tight). The pattern presented here is of traditional Japanese proportions, but feel free to alter the lines for a more comfortable fit. Another way around this problem is to use a knit or other stretch fabric and make the *tabi* a tiny bit smaller than called for. It's

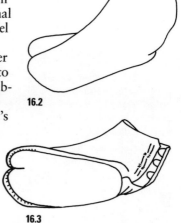

16.1

16.2

kohaze (clasp)

16.3

certainly worth the effort to make a test pair from cheap cotton or muslin so you can fine-tune the size first.

Materials

About ½ yard of 36″ fabric should be more than sufficient for the inpieces and outpieces for one pair of any size *tabi*. An equal amount of lining (any smooth, lightweight fabric) is required. Solid white, black, and navy blue are the usual colors, and silk (pongee or *habotae*) and cotton broadcloth are the standard outer fabrics.

About ¼ yard of heavy cotton, such as duck, and an equal amount of lining are needed for the bottom piece. White is the usual color for the face fabric. The traditional *tabi* maker would simultaneously preshrink and size the heavy cotton by boiling it in starch. It was then blocked out flat and allowed to dry thoroughly before cutting. This process made the fabric easier to work with (the edges would resist raveling) and longer wearing.

For the back closing, heavy button or upholstery thread and six *kohaze* clasps (three per sock) are required. *Kohaze* may be purchased in Japan or removed from old, worn-out *tabi* obtained from Japanese friends or flea markets.

Ideas

Substitute buttons, snaps, hooks and eyes, or even Velcro for the *kohaze*. A closer facsimile may be found in bait-and-tackle shops among the supplies for making lures and flies; ask for "blades."

Use a synthetic-cotton blend for a longer-wearing sole if you intend to wear the *tabi* around the house without any shoes or slippers on (as the Japanese do). For variety on top of the sock, try such fabrics as velvet, satin, corduroy, gabardine, lace, or even glove-weight leather. Thin flannel makes a soft lining.

Express playfulness with vivid colors, such as red, aqua, and moss green, and unexpected patterns, such as checks, paisley, stripes, and ikat designs. Fake animal fur patterns are perfect for making slippers.

Tabi are best suited for wear as slippers or as socks with any shoes or sandals that have a thong between the big toe and the other toes. Or you can hark back to ancient times and make the *tabi* with no split and wear them with regular shoes.

INSTRUCTIONS

1. Stand upright on a blank piece of paper with your full weight on your feet. Have a friend trace around each foot with a pencil held perpendicular to the paper at all times. Since a person's feet are often different sizes, be sure to trace each foot separately. Cut out each foot and label them "left" and "right."

2. Enlarge Figure 16.4 on a copy machine until it is the same length as your left-foot tracing. Keep track of how much you had to enlarge it (150%, 225%, etc.). Now enlarge Figures 16.5 and 16.6 by the same percentage. Label these pieces "left." Do not cut out these enlarged figures yet. Repeat this step for the right foot, using your right-foot tracing.

3. Now compare your original left-foot tracing with the enlarged bottom piece (Fig. 16.4). How does the width compare? If your tracing is a little narrower or wider, adjust the shape of the bottom piece accordingly (Figs. 16.7, 16.8). You may wish to alter the toe line as well. Repeat for the right foot, using your right-foot tracing.

Label, cut out, and use these corrected pattern pieces from now on. Left-foot and right-foot patterns should be mirror images of each other. It is not necessary to adjust the other pieces at this point.

4. Before cutting into your good fabric, test the fit of the

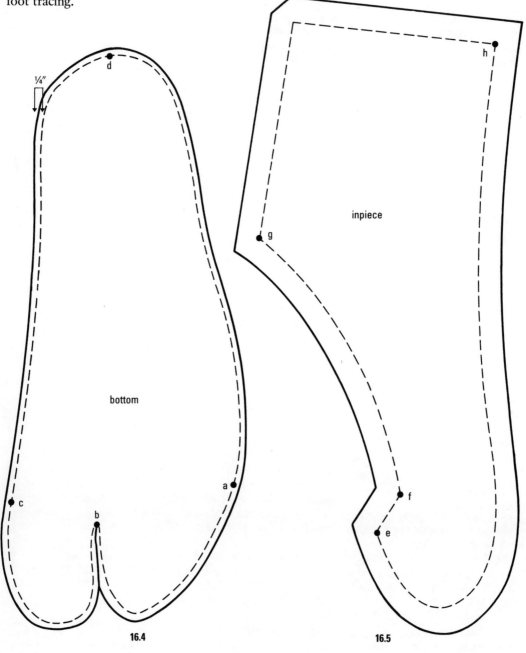

16.4

16.5

pattern pieces by following the rest of the instructions using an inexpensive fabric such as muslin. Don't worry about lining, finishing details, or quality construction for these test *tabi*.

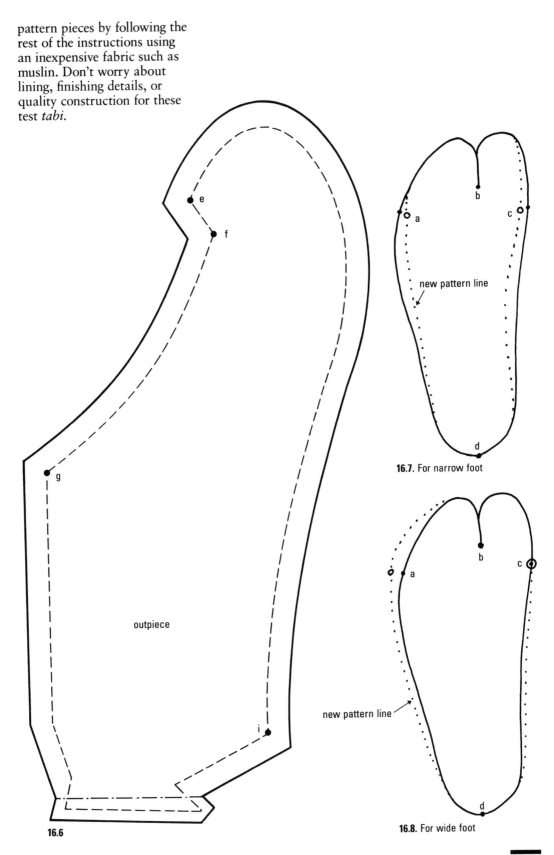

16.7. For narrow foot

new pattern line

new pattern line

outpiece

16.6

16.8. For wide foot

Tabi Socks

Try them on. The bottom piece should fit fine, but you may find that the *tabi* is tight or loose in other places. If the *tabi* is too tight across the top of your foot (a common problem with high arches), enlarge the outpiece and inpiece as shown in Figure 16.9. If the *tabi* is too loose across the top (typical for low arches), reduce these same pieces as shown in Figure 16.10.

If the sock is too loose or too tight around the ankle, alter the tops of the same pieces (Figs. 16.11, 16.12). Go through this process for both

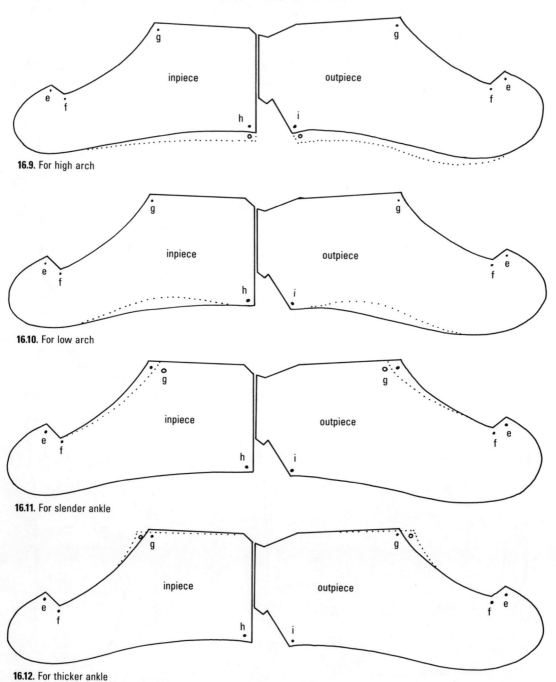

16.9. For high arch

16.10. For low arch

16.11. For slender ankle

16.12. For thicker ankle

feet to derive your final pattern pieces.

5. Cut out the inpiece and outpiece pattern pieces for each foot and label them. Pattern pieces for right foot should be mirror images of those for left foot.

6. Lay out all pattern pieces as follows: On your cutting surface, spread out the face fabric right-side *down*. Lay the lining, right-side *up*, on top of the face fabric. Pin the inpiece and outpiece patterns to both layers as shown in Figure 16.13. In a like manner, pin the bottom piece patterns to the heavier-weight fabric and lining (Fig. 16.13). Cut out all pieces.

7. Right sides together, sew the outpiece to the inpiece from *e* to *f* and then to *g*, taking a ¼″ seam allowance. (Note that all seam allowances for *tabi* are ¼″ unless otherwise indicated.) Clip the corner to point *f*. Press the seams open. Do this for the face fabric and the lining (Fig. 16.14).

8. Right sides together, sew the lining to the face fabric from point *g* in the directions of the arrows (Fig. 16.15). Trim off corners and turn right-side out.

9. Press all seam edges flat. With wrong sides together, machine-baste fabric and lining together, leaving a ⅛″ seam allowance, as shown in Figure 16.16. If any lining extends beyond the face fabric, trim it off.

If you intend to use buttons instead of *kohaze*, now is the time to add buttonholes to the outpiece. Fold the back flap to the lining side (Fig. 16.17) and sew the buttonholes through all layers (Fig. 16.18).

10. With wrong sides facing, machine-baste the bottom piece lining and fabric

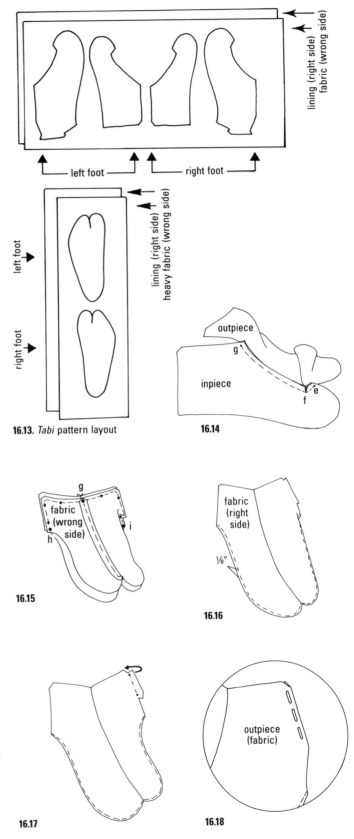

16.13. *Tabi* pattern layout

16.14

16.15

16.16

16.17

16.18

together, leaving a ⅛″ seam allowance all the way around.

11. Position point *i* on the out-piece so it overlaps point *h* on the inpiece by ½″. Tack securely at the bottom heel edge, sewing in a half-moon shape (Fig. 16.19). Turn *tabi* so lining faces out.

12. Align the tacked area with point *d* on the bottom piece, right sides of face fabric together. Sew between points *d* and *a*, going through all layers and leaving a ¼″ seam allowance (Fig. 16.20). Sew in a like manner from *d* to *c*.

13. On the outpiece, hand-baste from *a* to *e* about ⅛″ from the fabric edge. Pull the thread to gather the fabric until it fits the curve of the bottom piece (Fig. 16.21). Knot off the thread. Baste around the inpiece toe, from *e* to *c*, and ease to fit in the same manner. With right sides

together, machine-stitch the eased sections to the bottom piece.

14. Trim the seam allowance all around the bottom piece to ⅛″. Finish off the raw edges with machine zigzagging (Figs. 16.22, 16.23). Turn the *tabi* right-side out and press all edges.

15. To add the clasps, first press a fold in the outpiece flap as shown in Figure 16.17, lining sides together. Open the fold and position the clasps on the lining side of the flap (Fig. 16.24). Sew them in place with strong thread. Fold the flap back again and blindstitch in place (Fig. 16.25).

16. With sturdy thread, sew loops on the fabric side of the inpiece as shown in Figure 16.26. Tack down the strands in between the points where the *kohaze* clasps will hook under the two rows of thread.

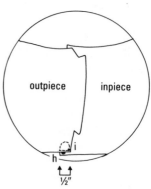

16.19

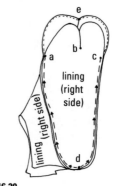

16.20

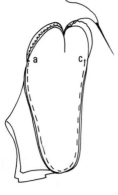

16.21

16.22

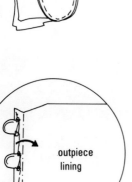...

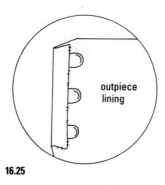

16.24

16.25

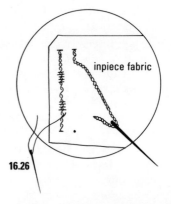

16.26

TABI SOCKS VARIATIONS

1. Traditional *jika-tabi*. To make, lengthen the top of the *tabi* to a comfortable height and add more *kohaze* at the back. Add parallel rows of topstitching around all seams for extra strength. Rubber soles in different sizes may be purchased in Japan at specialty stores catering to workmen. These soles are usually glued in place and then stitched down through prepunched holes around the sole edges.

2. *Tabi* shoes. For durability, thin leather has been sewn over the inpiece and outpiece, with windows designed to reveal the fabric below and enhance flexibility. The soles are tire retreads, cut to shape and glued with epoxy to the bottom. Buttons are used in place of *kohaze*.

Instead of leather, "plastic dip" may be applied to finished *tabi* to waterproof them for outdoor wear. Plastic dip, normally used to coat tool handles for a better grip, is available at large hardware stores. Use it with extreme care, as it is toxic.

3. Tall *tabi* with a front button closing.

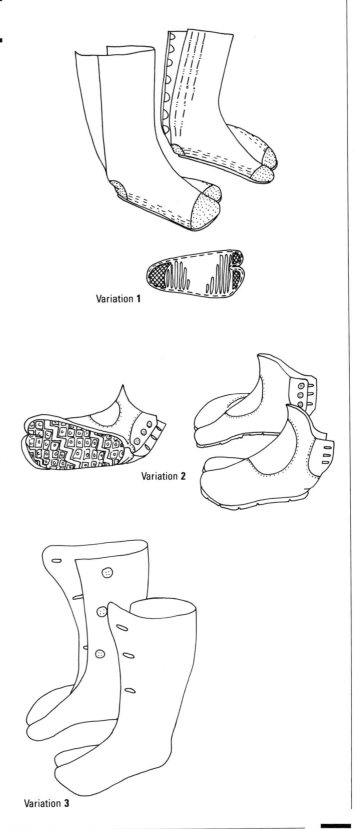

Variation **1**

Variation **2**

Variation **3**

Care and Storage

17 Care

In Japan, all handsewn kimono are completely unstitched before washing. The pieces are arranged and basted together so as to reconstruct the original bolt of fabric from which they were cut. This yardage is thoroughly laundered—spots are removed, faded areas are retouched—and a rice or seaweed sizing is applied to the clean fabric.

Then the weave is straightened and restretched to its original size by smoothing the wet fabric out on a long narrow board. When dry, the fabric is peeled off the board, the basting is removed, and the pieces are reassembled into a kimono.

As in premodern Europe, because of the time and labor involved, the outer layers of Japanese garments are washed infrequently—about once a year—so special care is taken to keep them clean.

This elaborate laundering process dramatically affects the long-term appearance of quality fabrics. At second-hand shops and flea markets you often see kimono that are puckered at the seams and just don't hang right. These kimono have been washed in their original stitched form. Since the Japanese usually do not preshrink the fabric and lining before construction, washing them together causes them to shrink at different

rates. There is nothing that can be done to remedy this problem short of unstitching the entire garment, washing and board-stretching the fabric, and sewing it back up again.

In Japan, specialty houses called *shiminuki-ya* spot-clean garments. The customer supplies the spot removal firm with as much information as possible, such as what dyes were used in the fabric, what was spilled, and so on. The spot remover, drawing on years of experience and family formulas, selects the proper combination of chemicals to remove the spot without harming the fabric. If it is necessary to remove some of the dyed color in the process, these professionals also have the expertise to redye the spot with a precise match.

Many Japanese do light spot-cleaning themselves each time they take off a traditional garment. This includes a light brushing to remove street dust and hanging the garment on a smooth straight pole to air before folding it away. Airing allows body moisture a chance to evaporate, extending the life of the fiber.

To launder a garment you have made, follow the instructions for the fabrics you used. If you preshrink both fabric and lining before cutting out the pattern, you should have no problem with uneven shrinking when laundering whole, stitched garments.

When machine-laundering, be careful about what other garments you throw in the washer at the same time. An open zipper on one garment may snag the delicate fabric of another.

Dry cleaning or gentle hand-washing (in baby shampoo) is recommended for handsewn garments. Most handsewing will not withstand rugged treatment. Many of the coarser silks may be machine-laundered and all silk may be hand-washed (except those dyed with noncolorfast dyes), but you should professionally dry-clean silk kimono made in Japan.

Extending the Garment's Life

After much wear, the cuff edges and hems of a kimono become worn or distressed. When this happens in Japan, the pieces are reassembled (after traditional laundering) in a different order, much like rotating the tires on a car for even wear. The side of the sleeve that forms the wrist area is resewn to the body. The body of the kimono is cut in half at the waist (the seam will later be concealed by the obi), and the fabric is turned upside down so that the middle becomes the hem and the (original) hem is sewn to the upper body at the waist.

The garments you fashion using this book may experience similar wear. If all the seams are machine-sewn, it is impractical to take apart the entire garment. You should, therefore, take preventative measures. For example, be sure to add the collar guard suggested with many garments. You might also use decorative patches similar to the collar guard in areas that wear or soil most often in your experience, especially if you intend to wear the garment often but wish to avoid frequent laundering. Incorporate the guards into the garment design.

Say, for example, you are designing a *hanten* jacket for a friend who works at a desk much of the time. Take into account his or her habits. If your friend uses the breast pockets a lot, be sure to reinforce them. Black velvet, with the nap pointing down, will add a luxurious touch, keep pencil and pen marks from showing, and prevent the pocket from wearing through.

Desk work also tends to soil and wear sleeve bottoms excessively. You might want to match the pocket lining with a decorative guard around the wrist opening, stitched on by hand so it can be easily replaced when worn out or removed when soiled.

These protective guards function much as leather elbow patches on tweed jackets or sweaters do. In fact, you may wish to add guards to the elbows of your friend's jacket. Guards around side pocket openings may also be called for. Use your imagination to devise creative solutions to your own particular design problems. Remember, too, that even if preventative measures are not taken, you can always add decorative patches over worn areas to extend the life of the garment at a later date.

Figures 17.1 and 17.2 show two jackets that incorporate protective guards into the garment design. A sewn version of Figure 17.2 is pictured on page 63.

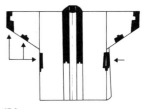

17.1

17.2

18 Storage

しまい方

Figures 18.1–27 show the various methods of folding traditionally constructed garments. Folding a garment and storing it in a drawer, instead of placing it on a hanger, helps prolong the life of the garment. Since most folds are along seams, there is no need to iron garments stored in this way.

However, when garments are to be stored for an extended period, key creases are often stitched into position. For example, the layers of each sleeve along the front and bottom edges are basted together ½" in from the edge; lined garments are basted together through all layers ½" above the bottom hem; and a *haori* collar is tacked flat against the jacket body.

The folded garment is wrapped in a storage envelope (*tato*) before being put away in a drawer or chest. These envelopes make it easier to look through several layers of garments without each becoming unfolded in the process. Directions for making your own storage envelopes are presented in the box on page 123.

When storing a garment away for a season or any extended period of time, you should protect it from insect damage. In the United States, moth balls are used for this purpose, but they have distinct disadvantages: They can

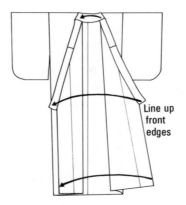

Line up front edges

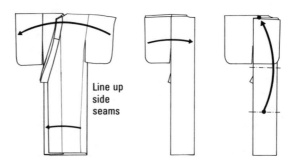

Line up side seams

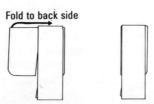

Fold to back side

18.1–6. How to fold a kimono, *yukata*, or outer robe

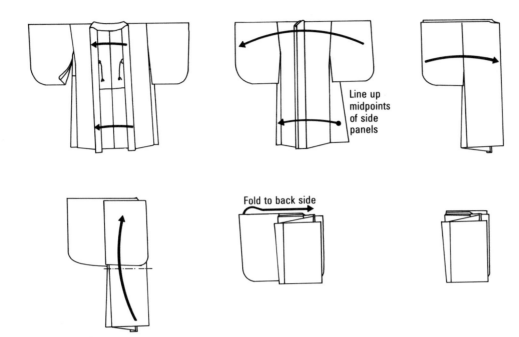

Line up
midpoints
of side
panels

Fold to back side

18.7–12. How to fold a *haori* jacket (pictured) or *hanten* jacket

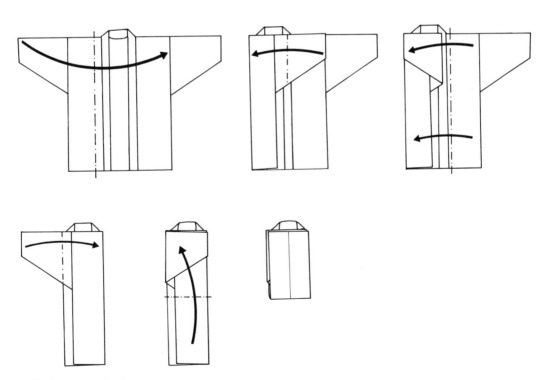

18.13–18. How to fold a *hanten* jacket (pictured) or wraparound top

be toxic to pets and humans as well as leave an unpleasant odor on garments long after they have been taken out of storage.

The Japanese usually pack clothing away in camphor chips. Each chip is about the size of a sugar cube. To use, break open the plastic wrapper around a cube and wrap the cube in a piece of facial tissue. Place the wrapped cube inside the storage envelope after a garment has been inserted. Use one cube per envelope. The porosity of the tissue allows the fumes to escape slowly.

Camphor has a pleasant smell (to humans) that repels insects without killing them. This nontoxicity makes camphor safe for use in households with small children or pets. In addition, the scent disappears from garments soon after removing them from storage, usually within 1 to 2 hours. Camphor chips can be found in many Japanese pharmacies and variety stores (both in Japan and in Japantowns abroad). Ask for *shono* or *shono seizai*.

Begin with obi folded in thirds.

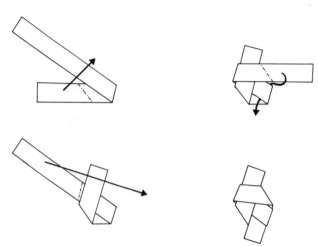

18.19–23. How to fold a *kaku* obi

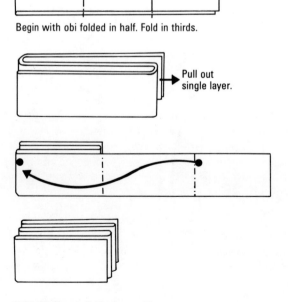

Begin with obi folded in half. Fold in thirds.

Pull out single layer.

18.24–27. How to fold a *maru* obi

STORAGE ENVELOPES

High-quality handmade paper is used to make storage envelopes for traditional clothing in Japan, but you may substitute clean white butcher paper.

1. Place the folded garment on a large sheet of paper. Measure a small margin (1″–3″) around it to determine the size of the bottom panel. Sketch flaps extending from each side of the bottom panel as shown in Figure 1. Flaps *a* and *b* should be about one-third the length of the bottom panel. Flaps *c* and *d* should be about the same size as the bottom panel. Cut out the paper.

2. Twisted Japanese paper is used for the ties in Japan, but you may substitute soft packaging cord or ribbon if you like. Cut six pieces, each 8″–10″ in length.

3. Cut tiny slits in the envelope at the approximate positions indicated and insert about 1″ of each twisted paper or cord piece through to the inside. (If using twisted paper, untwist the end to keep it from slipping back through. Cord can be secured with a simple knot in the end or unraveled and splayed a bit.)

4. Glue each short cord end to the paper with white glue or paper paste. Cover the raw end by gluing a small square of colored paper on top of it. Allow to dry.

5. To keep the cut corners from ripping during handling, paste triangular paper reinforcements at the corners as shown, overlapping the paper edge by ¼″. A contrasting color adds a decorative touch to the envelope.

Although not traditional, you may find it convenient to paste a sheet of Bristol board to the inside bottom of the envelope, ½″ smaller all the way around than the bottom itself. This lends extra body to the package, making it easier to handle.

6. On the outside of flap *d* (the top flap when the envelope is tied), paste a rectangular piece of white or light-colored paper. On this label indicate the contents of the envelope (for example, "blue kimono") so you won't have to open it to determine what's inside. Sometimes a square hole is cut in the envelope and a cellophane panel is pasted over it; this window allows instant identification of the envelope's contents.

7. To use, place the garment on the bottom panel, fold flaps *a* and *b* in to the center, and tie the cords in a loose square knot (Fig. 2). Fold flaps *c* and *d* to the center and tie the cords into loose simple bows (Fig. 3). These envelopes can be stacked on top of one another in a drawer or chest.

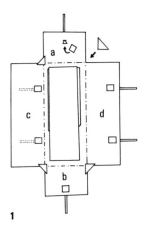

1

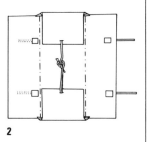

2

3

Metric Conversion Charts

Converting Decimal Fractions to Inches

A pocket calculator yields decimal fractions, which is fine if you are plotting your pattern in metric measurements, but cumbersome when it comes to inches. Below is a chart of decimal equivalents of commonly used inch fractions. Select the decimal fraction closest to the one you are trying to convert, and use the inch equivalent given.

.0625 = $\frac{1}{16}$"
.125 = $\frac{1}{8}$"
.1875 = $\frac{3}{16}$"
.25   = $\frac{1}{4}$"
.3125 = $\frac{5}{16}$"
.375 = $\frac{3}{8}$"
.5   = $\frac{1}{2}$"
.5625 = $\frac{9}{16}$"
.625 = $\frac{5}{8}$"
.6875 = $\frac{11}{16}$"
.75   = $\frac{3}{4}$"
.8125 = $\frac{13}{16}$"
.875 = $\frac{7}{8}$"
.9375 = $\frac{15}{16}$"

Converting Metric Measurements to Inches (and Vice Versa)

Readers in Japan or other countries that use the metric system may wish to convert all the measurements in this book to the metric system (though it would be simpler to purchase a measuring tape calibrated in inches). Likewise, if you think in inches but find yourself purchasing fabric in Japan, the second chart below may come in handy.

Approximate Conversions from Metric Measures

When You Know	Multiply by	To Find
millimeters	.04	inches
centimeters	.4	inches
meters	3.3	feet

Approximate Conversions to Metric Measures

When You Know	Multiply by	To Find
inches	25	millimeters
inches	2.5	centimeters
feet	30	centimeters
yards	.9	meters

INCHES   CENTIMETERS

Sources of Supplies

FABRIC

As any textiles addict knows, there is no end to the supply of fabrics. The trick is to find the right one at the right price for the purpose at hand, whether it be a flea market bonanza (a plastic-backed brocade curtain, say, for dyeing and transformation into a Japanese-style raincoat) or an exquisite silk weave. Check your local fabric stores, upholstery shops, and, yes, flea markets for unusual fabrics. Some sources of silks and Japanese fabrics are listed here, as well as two sources of fabrics suitable for surface decoration (Cerulean Blue and Testfabrics).

CERULEAN BLUE, LTD.
P.O. Box 21168
Seattle, WA 98111
(206)443-7744

Natural-fiber fabrics (cotton, silk, rayon) prepared for dyeing and printing, fabric dyes and paints, Japanese dye brushes and tools. Mail order only.

EXOTIC SILKS!
1959 B Leghorn
Mountain View, CA 94043
(800)845-7455
(800)345-7455 (California)

Wholesale outlet for Thai Silks! (see below). Stocks a wide range of quality silks and other fibers at very low prices. Mail order only. Minimum cut: 15 yards.

HORIKOSHI NEW YORK, INC.
55 West 39th Street
New York, NY 10018
(212)354-0133

Wide range of quality Japanese silks and other fabrics, including Japanese weaves in Western widths. Reasonable prices. Wholesale and retail. Mail order welcome.

KASURI DYEWORKS
1959 Shattuck Avenue
Berkeley, CA 94704
(415)841-4509

Specializes in narrow width (14"–16") fabric imported from Japan: in particular, ikat (*kasuri*) and tie-dyed (*shibori*) weaves and cotton prints for *yukata*. Good selection. Also carries *sashiko* embroidery thread and books on Japanese needle arts. Videos on such subjects as Japanese tie-dying, ikat, and stencil cutting are for sale or may be viewed on the premises. Mail order welcome.

KIMONO MY HOUSE
1424 62nd Street
Emeryville, CA 94608
(415)654-4627

Treasure trove of used kimono
and just about everything
wearable from Japan. Slightly
damaged pieces are ideal, eco-
nomical source of traditional
Japanese textiles for resewing
into new garments. Also available are *haori* ties, sewing
chests, obi and hair orna-
ments, *jika-tabi*, etc. Retail
and wholesale. Hours are
irregular so call for information first.

ORIENTAL SILK CO.
8375–77 Beverly Boulevard
Los Angeles, CA 90048
(213)651-2323

Good selection of silks, sold
both retail and wholesale.
Mail order welcome.

TESTFABRICS, INC.
P.O. Box 420
Middlesex, NJ 08846
(201)469-6446

Untreated fabrics ideal for
printing, dyeing, and painting
(or for use by people with
allergies). Mail order welcome.

THAI SILKS!
252 State Street
Los Altos, CA 94022
(415)948-8611

Retail and discount outlet. No
mail order. Has wonderful
remnant selection. (See also
Exotic Silks! above.)

THOUSAND CRANES
FUTON SHOP
1803 4th Street
Berkeley, CA 94710
(415)849-0501

Wide range of Japanese textiles and other imported fabrics that reflect Japanese
tastes, such as Guatemalan
ikats and Marimekko fabrics.

UTEX TRADING
710 9th Street, Suite 5
Niagara Falls, NY 14301
(416)596-7565, ext. 38

Good range of silks at reasonable prices. Mail order only.

SEWING TOOLS

The Japanese "third hand"
is often available through
mail-order ads placed in sewing magazines. Japanese sewing chests are carried by
dealers in Japanese chests
(*tansu*) or furniture.

CLOTILDE, INC.
1909 S.W. First Avenue
Fort Lauderdale, FL 33315
(305)761-8655

Sells "third hands" and other
Japanese sewing tools. Mail
order only.

PROFESSIONAL SEWING
SUPPLIES
P.O. Box 14272
Seattle, WA 98114
(206)324-8823

Better-quality sewing supplies,
including "third hands," silk
thread, and Japanese needles.
Wholesale and retail. Mail
order only.

UWAJIMAYA, INC.
P.O. Box 3003
Seattle, WA 98114
(206)624-6248

Carries Japanese thimbles,
scissors, and marking styluses,
as well as a wide selection of
Japanese craft books. Mail
order welcome.

Further Reading

Blakemore, Frances. *Japanese Design Through Textile Patterns*. Tokyo: John Weatherhill, 1978.

Ekiguchi, Kunio, and Ruth S. McCreery. *A Japanese Touch for the Seasons*. Tokyo: Kodansha International, 1987. Includes instructions for making a traditional Japanese thimble, as well as several sewing projects for the home.

Ito, Toshiko. *Tsujigahana: The Flower of Japanese Textile Art*. Tokyo: Kodansha International, 1981.

Japan Textile Color Design Center, comp. *Okinawan, Ainu and Foreign Designs*. Vol. 3 of *Textile Designs of Japan*. Tokyo: Kodansha International, 1981.

Kolander, Cheryl. *A Silk Worker's Notebook*. Loveland, Colorado: Interweave Press, 1985.

Koren, Leonard. *New Fashion Japan*. Tokyo: Kodansha International, 1984.

Minnich, Helen Benton. *Japanese Costume and the Makers of Its Elegant Tradition*. Rutland, Vermont: Charles E. Tuttle, 1963.

Nakano, Eisha, with Barbara Stephan. *Japanese Stencil Dyeing*. Tokyo: John Weatherhill, 1982.

Stinchecum, Amanda Mayer. *Kosode: Sixteenth to Nineteenth Century Textiles from the Nomura Collection*. Tokyo: Kodansha International, 1984.

Wada, Yoshiko, Mary Kellogg Rice, and Jane Barton. *Shibori: The Inventive Art of Japanese Shaped Resist-Dyeing*. Tokyo: Kodansha International, 1984. [check date]

Yamanaka, Norio. *The Book of Kimono*. Tokyo: Kodansha International, 1982.

Yamanobe, Tomoyuki, ed. *Opulence: The Kimonos and Robes of Itchiku Kubota*. New York: Kodansha International, 1984.

Index

Acknowledgments

I would like to express my appreciation for all the work Pamela Pasti has put into this project. It is through her efforts as editor that this book has developed beyond a hodgepodge of ideas and text. I also wish to express my deep-felt gratitude to Katsuko Kanematsu: In sharing her love of Japanese clothing and design she helped fire my interest in textiles, while encouraging me in my search for a better understanding of Japanese culture.

In addition, thanks go to Kunio Ekiguchi for guiding me in my studies; Machiko Moriyasu for her research assistance; Kimono My House for generously loaning props for the color photographs; Susan Parrish for her assistance with the photographs; and Naomi Goto for her enthusiastic support.

The models in the photographs are: Theresa Hamilton, Adee Wada, Sierra Stevens-McGeever, Susan Barnard-Sasaki, Liesa Lietzke, Charles Arenson, Lucille Arenson, and Janice Fujii.